SOUNDINGS
AT SEA LEVEL

HENRY BEETLE HOUGH

SOUNDINGS

AT SEA LEVEL

Drawings by Donald Carrick

HOUGHTON MIFFLIN COMPANY BOSTON

1980

Library of Congress Cataloging in Publication Data
Hough, Henry Beetle, date
    Soundings at sea level.

    1. Hough, Henry Beetle, 1896–   —Biography.
2. Authors, American—20th century—Biography.
3. Journalists—United States—Biography. I. Title.
PS3515.075933Z465   070.4′092′4 [B]   80–10802
ISBN 0–395–29165–8

Printed in the United States of America

v 10 9 8 7 6 5 4 3 2 1

TO THE THREE GRAHAMS
IMPORTANT IN MY LIFE

SOUNDINGS
AT SEA LEVEL

WHEN GRAHAM AND I were at Starbuck's Neck this morning in the sweet chill of late October air, the last morning but one before another term of Daylight Saving would expire, the full moon hung in the sky above the old Wimpenney house so exactly that it could have been taken for a marker. We had started out with a flashlight for passage through the darkness of the wooded path on this side of Sheriff's Meadow Pond, and sunrise was still a good twenty minutes off when we reached the Neck, but now the light had come up from below the horizon and was brightening the moon into a condition of more than ordinary splendor.

Graham and I turned several times as we walked along the causeway toward the Harbor Light and looked back at the moonscape of the town, which seemed to be raised up handsomely because of our distance from it and our almost sea level of observation. Given a harbor to front upon, Edgartown had by common purpose presented to it a choice of serene and thrifty white houses inhabited by the appropriate spirit of seafaring. Only the Victorian jumble of the Harbor View Hotel at the easternmost end of North Water Street had exempted itself from the old fashion, emphasizing its enterprise dating from 1891 and an ostentation in its claim upon new times, the newest of which it perhaps looked upon with surprise.

We saw the white houses emerge through a succession of auroral changes that tinted their expressions and brought the shadows of porches and chimneys into different attitudes and definitions, setting off the treetops into patterns of fretted gilt. A word occurred to me for the precise glow of the moon — "valorous" — and I did not reject it because it was private with me and so candid a pathetic fallacy. Ruskin, who invented that phrase, used it as much as anyone before or since.

So came another morning to Starbuck's Neck, and I was glad that we were at that exact place as witnesses. Graham's thought remained obscure, but he looked at me and then at what I seemed to be looking at. After consideration that seemed to satisfy him, he went on with an examination of the causeway rocks and herbage, mostly tattered goldenrod, beach grass, and beach roses — actually *Rosa rugosa* — that bore plump red fruits and a second blooming of red or white flowers at the same time, one of our many salutes to fall.

Graham is my collie, friend and companion, on many occasions the master of my time and purposes. We keep house together — not alone, since no man with a dog is alone, or the other way around, either — pooling our interests and resources. He is now seven and weighs about ninety pounds, including the wind-blown abundance of his rough collie coat. Mostly it is copper-colored, but with accents of black and a white blaze between alert brown eyes. I am astonished to remember that I could lift him with one hand when I first brought him home, and that we both slept in one single bed.

Things I used to expect him to know, he now expects me to know, and if I overlook them, he reminds me. He initiates changes in the walks we take together and sometimes adds a mile to the distance, but we never differ as to the region. This morning he led me through Ox Pond Meadow instead of through Cottage Street. His judgment was a wise one.

Late this afternoon I heard him howling outside our front door as if the day of the Lord was at hand (Isaiah 13:6), the sound he makes when he puts his head far up and back, jaws wide, and uses all the resources of throat and lungs for the soaring of high, fluctuating notes. I opened the door and found him standing on the porch quite casually, desiring only to be let in, and no slouching around about it. I had never known him to howl that way except as a reprise to the siren of the police cruiser or ambulance.

If our morning visits to Starbuck's Neck could be separated by miles instead of hours, Graham and I would be travelers afar, so far that I cannot imagine the remoteness. Thoreau wanted his companion to give some evidence that he had traveled farther than the sources of the Nile. I am sure Graham would have qualified. Yet we both remain securely in the territories of home, and always on foot, this last the very ideal of voyaging. Time must be the dimension of our only strict reality and we cross its meridians with wider vistas because Starbuck's Neck is a storied place with associations running long ago and to the ends of the earth.

Here in the predawn twilight, and a little later when the red sun appears, I might claim to meet the old familiars of the Neck, I feel their presence so convincingly. They would be as weightless as shadows, yet trudging in their former habit at a pace common to their days. I might meet them in snow, wind, rain, or in those special interludes when tranquillity exists untouched as it did this morning. I think I would know them well, though most of them I never met face to face: Captain Joseph Swasey and his daughter Faustina; Captain Robert Wimpenney, Daniel Fellows with the fancy waistcoat and silvered hair of a small-town squire; and surely Captain Eric Gabrielson of strong, weathered face and solid habit of command, and Major Charles J. Allen of the Army Engineers, recently arrived from flood control on the rolling Mississippi and eager to put down the tap root of a new era of summer people on Starbuck's Neck, above the coming and going of our tides.

Such meetings I cannot pretend to be other than fantasy, but nevertheless I am ready to give long odds on their historic authenticity. "All power of fancy over reason is a degree of insanity," wrote Dr. Johnson. Perhaps so, but much reason needs outside help, just as "the fullness of professional knowledge might need the supplement of quackery." I copied this from a book, but cannot remember what book and am powerless to give decent credit.

Graham and I walked along the causeway to the big

rock, beyond which only a track of loose sand leads the few remaining yards to the Harbor Light, in the lantern of which, atop a graceful white tower, the intermittent red flashes would soon beg off and die. We verified again most of the particulars of the view, each to his own taste, and turned to walk back toward the town.

In times past, even within my own generation, there had been deep water close in to shore, deep enough on one occasion for a sailing vessel to lie against the bank and discharge lumber for the building of the old Wimpenney house. This event would have been just before or after 1796, the year in which Captain Joseph Swasey, believed to have been born José de Souza in Lisbon, took Susanna Pease of Edgartown for his bride.

Close above the shore, opposite the new house, stood the saltworks, with vats like extended, rather narrow and shallow boxes, the sides five or six inches deep, raised on posts about three feet above the ground. The length of the vats, surprising to the eye, made lines of perspective that were repeated in shadows on sunny days, except that at equinoctial noons the shadows would retreat under the greater boldness of the vats themselves. At other times they observed a geometry decreed by the physics of light and its cycles of angularity.

Salt water, pumped from the harbor into the vats, would be evaporated by the sun's heat — solar energy, as it is best known today — and the residue of salt, with trace elements of desirable and rare kinds, would be scraped out for domestic use or to salt the town's catch of certain fish, including the great quantity of alewives dipped in spring from the Mattakessett Creek. Covers, fixed on rollers, protected the vats in case of rain.

Technology has never produced installations more satisfying to the eye than such old time saltworks, not even the more greatly extended ropewalks, which were, offsetting their length, too clumsy and solid for any real grace of perspective. Moreover, the wood of the saltworks, planks and posts, took on a character much like that of ships' timbers. They were weathered and weathered again, and sustained splendid wounds that affirmed their strength.

The passing of the era of deep water along this shore occurred in the 1930s when a blight destroyed the meadows of eel grass that had stabilized the sea bottom throughout all remembered generations. Without this underwater truce between submerged earth and sea, the will of tide, wind, and storm prevailed unchecked, especially in the wild northeasters of winter. The bottom sands stirred, shifted, marched eastward in a force of conquest, so that if the present causeway had not been built to replace the old wooden bridge to the lighthouse, Edgartown harbor would have been shoaled seriously. The rock causeway served as a breakwater, and against it some broad acres of sand, perhaps five or six, accumulated offshore in a crescent from the Harbor Light around the curve of Starbuck's Neck.

Separating this new region of sand and beach grass from the old shore of the Neck, a lagoon had formed, though some who were unversed in such matters carelessly referred to it as a salt pond. It was no pond. It was a lagoon, such as Conrad and Robert Louis Stevenson wrote about, but in our colder region formed not by coral but by an arm of sand, shaped by tide and winds, stealing around and enclosing a captive loop of sea. Captain Robert Wimpenney knew such lagoons in the South Seas, and so did many wives of Edgartown who sailed to the Pacific with their husbands. "Like flame, like wine, across the still lagoon, /

the colors of the sunset stream": This, by William Rose
Benét, suited me very well, though my chosen time was
that of sunrise.

The original shoreline itself remained a lowland of salt
marsh, varied with elevations of solid ground, relic of an
estuary into which flowed the rains of Starbuck's Neck,
filtered through sand and clay, to mix at last with tidal salt
water. The apron of lowland extended from the base of the
high bank, below the street, to the irregular rim of the
lagoon, a margin made smooth by the bordering growth
of beach grass and kindred plants. All this was opposite
the Harbor View, which both squatted and towered in
ambiguous, turn-of-the-centry fashion, depending on
whether one looked upon its gables or the bay windows
that avoided, of all things, symmetry.

This is what Graham and I saw as we retraced our steps
along the causeway: the outer beach and sandy continent
in extreme miniature, its reach extending beyond our vision
as it turned and faced upon Vineyard Sound rather than
the harbor; the harbor itself, and the boats of fishermen;
ahead of us the town, and behind us now the Harbor Light,
the entrance strait, and the morning sky.

Graham left me for a route along the beach, while I
chose the parallel street above, under the trees, each of us
knowing we would meet again at the Cottage Street corner.

A harbor entrance in former times was important to
everyone by right of its birthright, scenery, symbolism,
and role in the life of mariners and in the push of enterprise. Expectancy is still an inherent attribute, never quite
dormant, affecting landsmen and coastal people alike because it is so interwoven with many strands of human
experience.

Between the separating arms of land is the movement of the tides, the active principle of coming and going, arrival and departure, giving or being given, taking or losing. With this special prospect and its mythos I identify the migration of Captain Joseph Swasey from Lisbon prior to 1766. Susanna Pease, whom he married, was a daughter of John Pease, removed by three generations from an original John Pease, a settler of 1642. Whatever else Susanna gave to her bridegroom, she conveyed the pride and tradition of an already venerable family of the port. She joined him to the Establishment.

Joseph and Susanna had daughters named Betsy, Susanna, Mary, Elizabeth, Juliana, Hepsibah, Clarissa and — a departure from the familiar christenings of the place and time — Faustina. An earlier, distant Faustina had been the wife of Antoninus Pius, and another was the wife of Marcus Aurelius. I wonder by what tie of chance or blood or association this name came from Rome to Lisbon and at last to Starbuck's Neck for use by the sixth daughter and eighth child of Joseph and Susanna Swasey.

Faustina Swasey married Captain Robert Wimpenney on May 3, 1798. He, at the age of thirty-eight, commanded ships in the China trade and, his grandson told me, served as his own supercargo, since he was of unusual attainments, and also enjoyed the privilege of admission to the walled cities of China. He was a lunarian and could navigate by the moon, and if necessary by the moon alone. His ship was lost with all on board, most likely in a typhoon in the China Sea. Faustina lived on as a widow in the house Captain Robert had built for her, next to that of her father, whose dwelling had become, in the familiar evolution of towns like ours, "the old Wimpenney house."

The Wimpenney houses had taken their places in the determined line on North Water Street facing the harbor, each house a jog or so out of parallel with its next neighbor, so that all would have a view of Cape Pogue and the harbor entrance. So resolute is this attentive posture of the houses that it arouses wonder and speculation among the town's visitors as year succeeds year.

Captain Robert Wimpenney left seven children, six sons and a daughter. Three of the sons were lost at sea, and of the other progeny only one met death on the land. Faustina eventually sold her house to Dr. Samuel Wheldon, physician and innkeeper, whose son-in-law, Captain John H. Pease, sailed in 1822 as first mate of the ship *Thames* of New London when it took the second batch of American missionaries out to the Sandwich Islands. A baby born on that voyage was named Seaforth.

In 1846, now master of the whaleship *Chandler Price* of New Bedford, Captain Pease happened upon some floating wreckage in the Pacific, traced it by tidal evidence to Sydenham's Island, and rescued survivors of the wrecked *Columbia* who were living in peril and hardship. In all he sailed sixteen voyages, discovered uncharted Pacific shoals, never drank a glass of liquor or smoked a pipe or cigar, but quarreled publicly with a dentist about the fit of his wife's false teeth.

Another shipmaster who lived in that block of North Water Street, only a little removed from Starbuck's Neck, was Captain Edwin Coffin who, in his youth, had sailed as a noncommissioned officer in the navy. The vessel with five hundred men on board was threatened with grounding on a lee shore in a gale of wind, the peril each moment more grave. The anguished, hesitant commander said to young Coffin, "What would you do?"

"If I had a whaleboat's crew I would put her out to sea."

"Can you put her out to sea?"

"Yes, sir."

"The ship is in your charge. I want you to put her out to sea."

"Yes, sir."

The gale and raging seas notwithstanding, young Coffin got the ship safely out beyond the hazard of the lee shore. He then presented himself to the captain.

"Your ship is at sea, sir."

This dialogue seems a little stilted over a long formalism of time, but I had it word for word more than once from Theodore S. Wimpenney, himself veteran of a whaling voyage and grandson of Captain Robert Wimpenney.

In later years Captain Edwin Coffin sailed to the Pacific as master of the *Joseph Meigs* of New Bedford and headed a polar expedition that, like many others, did not reach the Pole. So much, and I hope not too much, is offered in documentation of the oceanic character of North Water Street and Starbuck's Neck.

Dr. Wheldon sold his house to Captain Francis J. Silva, who was born in Fayal, westernmost of the gray Azores that Joaquin Miller wrote about, though Vineyard seamen always found them green and abloom with gay flowers. In 1885 Captain Silva sold the house to Captain Eric Gabrielson who was marrying Mary Belle Wimpenney, granddaughter of Captain Robert.

Captain Gabrielson paid $400 for the property, a sum that makes him distant from the present day by about $150,000, as well as by ninety-three years, computed according to the date of purchase. Here, of course, inflation plays a role, but so too with time, which is a dimension, not a uniform standard at all, and in fact accelerates its course from Cathay to Fleet Street to Broadway to Starbuck's

Neck, as well as from Gutenberg to Merganthaler to the laser beam, or from *Acta Diurna* to the *New York Times* to the *Vineyard Gazette*.

Captain Gabrielson was born in Stavanger, Norway, a port on Stavanger Fjord that opens into Bokn Fjord, where the Bay of Dusovik served as a rendezvous for vessels of war. I think the captain was in a true sense a Viking, and he wore the blue of the United States Navy and Coast Guard for more than forty years. He commanded a revenue cutter when, at the age of twenty-seven, he married Mary Belle.

His house now sits in the row of staunch and commanding white houses at which I look with appreciation in early mornings throughout the year, a hip roof next to a pitched roof, chimneys varied in size, the most substantial ones painted white with tapering black caps. One pauses here, looking out over the harbor and listening to the roll and beat of ocean surf pounding out its turbulence, or the more deliberate old swell of some distant storm on the East Beach of Chappaquiddick.

〰

I come now to a portentous change in the life and times of Starbuck's Neck, amounting in earthly terms to an apotheosis but not genuinely an exaltation. Change occurred slowly at first, no thought yet of an unending traffic of sightseeing buses and the Age of Strangers. What happened was that General Allen and his wife chose a site at the end of North Water Street for that historic monument, the first house built in Edgartown expressly for a summer sojourner and off-Islander. Summer visitors there had been, often bound in loyalty by marriage to a Vineyard bride, so that someday it might be said the town was marrying into a new century. This meant no commitment to change, since

the attachment was to the existing order and the old quality of life, but change all the same was implicit in what
one did and how one went on from here.

Judge George B. Young, who had been general counsel
to the Great Northern Railroad prior to his elevation to the
Supreme Court of Minnesota, visited Martha's Vineyard
and married Ellen Olivia Fellows, daughter of Daniel Fellows, Esq., clerk of the court of common pleas of Edgartown.

When Judge Young held court in St. Paul, he and Ellen
met and became friends of Major Charles J. Allen and Mrs.
Allen. The major was then occupied with his Mississippi
River work. From the Youngs, the Allens heard much
about Edgartown and were encouraged to see the town for
themselves. One visit led to another, until in 1882 the
Vineyard Gazette published this report.

> Mrs. Charles J. Allen of St. Paul, Minnesota, has just pur-
> chased of Mrs. Parnell C. Pease one-fourth of an acre of
> land at the east end of North Water Street, adjoining the
> residence of Jeremiah Pease, Esq., and will have a cottage
> erected there before another season. This land, overlooking
> both harbor and Sound, is part of the premises on which
> there has been talk for so many years of erecting a hotel,
> and is one of the most eligible sites for a summer residence
> in the whole township.

Not then did the reference to a summer hotel seem much
of an omen, one way or another. The Allens built, and
what they built was the prototype and symbol of a trans-
formed civilization, a summer cottage. They left space in
front for expansion of the cottage into that newer symbol, a
"colonial house," but the space remained as a front yard,
the only one of the kind on the street.

Grace Allen was to write a good many years later that the cottage grew at the sides and rear, less ambitiously but more practically. It had two stories, a modified gambrel roof limiting the space in the upper story, and a roofed veranda across the front, styled differently from the older and smaller porticoes on the street. An intentional modesty about it has persisted through the years, together with a sunny, vacationing character and genuine innocence.

When Dick Shute, former Civil War drummer boy and now the town photographer, aimed his camera from under the new porch roof, its lens viewed nothing beyond but open land, treeless on account of the windy exposure, natively bare, with the varying aspects of sea and sky off beyond. Later there would be a fence over which Rodolphus Pease's cows would put their heads to stare at young Grace Allen as they ruminated on summer days.

In Grace's childhood the neighboring Jeremiah Pease house had become the John Wesley Pease house. John Wesley had married the widow VanDusen, upon whom he had been calling every Saturday night with the same regularity of his trips on Sunday with flowers to put on his father's grave. Mrs. Pease became "Aunt Lucy" to Grace Allen, a rewarding complimentary kinship.

Once John Wesley said to Lucy, "I saw Mrs. Allen walking on the lighthouse bridge in a breeze. She has the prettiest legs in Edgartown."

"Oh, Johnny, what an awful thing to say!"

"Aunt Lucy I dearly loved," Grace Allen told me in years long afterward. "She used to bring things to eat, and I can still see her beyond our hollyhocks. Once she called to me, 'Gracie, here are some johnny-cakes. Ministers always like johnny-cakes.' I remember the silver coffin plates mounted on black velvet and framed in Aunt Lucy's parlor, next to the sitting room, and I saw her there for the last time. She took my hand and said, 'Good-by, Gracie, we will meet the other side of Jordan.' "

Long absent from Edgartown, in a newer, different time, Grace wrote a poem, changing names, but remembering Aunt Lucy:

> Between our garden and the Norton place
> the hollyhocks swayed by the picket fence
> and always there were rows of heliotrope,
> four o'clocks and sweet alyssum,
> ribbons of color on the ground.
> I remember still.
>
> I remember how the Captain's widow,
> Aunt Sarah, as we used to say, would call
> across the hollyhocks, "I saw just now
> your minister go in. They all
> like johnny-cakes, the ministers."
> I took the warm plate.

Then the theme of the late captain, how he fed sea gulls in winter and talked of Pacific islands:

> There was a day when I, a child, went in
> The darkened parlor with the funeral wreath,
> waxen flowers beneath a dome of glass,
> framed in black velvet hung against
> faded wallpaper
>
> There, lying in a bed moved from her room,
> was Mrs. Norton. She whispered, "Good-by,
> We will meet again upon the other
> side of Jordan. The Captain said . . ."
> I heard the sea gulls and wondered
> What the Captain said.

The *Saturday Review* accepted this poem, but John Ciardi, who was modern and advanced, became poetry editor and refused to publish it. This is how poetry has been taken away from the people, even from those who have not yet found it really within their grasp. So we published the poem in the *Vineyard Gazette*. This was in 1965, and we thought we could hear Aunt Lucy's voice even at such a remove, as of course John Ciardi couldn't.

The Allens named their cottage "Sea Rest," a Starbuck's Neck adaptation of a major's, then a colonel's, and finally a general's dream of retirement.

Mrs. Allen was received with friendship among the townspeople, simply and naturally by her neighbors. Judge Young and General Allen joined the Home Club, no bar against summer visitors, along with mariners, fishermen, and town dignitaries. An equality of individual merit and geniality prevailed, geniality being the quality most prized. But the Allens and Youngs also walked the length of Water Street for social calls upon each other's households, a custom indicating that evolution of a summer colony had begun.

It was held against summer people almost from the beginning that they wanted to change things, to tell you what you ought to do, and even to take charge. Mrs. Allen was close on the line when she introduced services of the Episcopalian denomination to Edgartown, where many thought that the Methodist, Baptist, and original Congregational Churches were quite enough.

The first Episcopal communion, as remembered by Grace, was held at Sea Rest, the Reverend William Cleveland Hicks, rector of Grace Episcopal Church of Vineyard Haven, coming down to officiate. Services were then transferred to Gothic Hall, a spacious second-floor area upstairs over Captain Jethro Cottle's dry-goods store on Main Street, formerly used by Enoch Cornell as a tintype parlor and ice-cream saloon. Tall, pointed windows looked down upon the street, and still do, though the street has changed its nature.

Hattie Shute, sister of Dick, the photographer, presided at the organ, as the saying was, and I wonder what type of organ it may have been. A "parlor" type, I suppose, the organist's seat finished in red wool embroidered with birds, flowers, or a dream of Jerusalem. Every Sunday morning Hattie played "Eternal Father, strong to save, whose arm hath bound the restless wave," until finally she felt good and tired of it. Then one climactic Sunday she rose at the conclusion of the service and said, "Not any more!", her dark eyes flashing and her lips coming resolutely together. I know how it was, because for many years we were contemporaries of Hattie, and many a boiled dinner I watched her eat at Hallowell's Restaurant on hot summer days when she was living in widowhood alone.

Across the street from Sea Rest, at a short remove, stood the house of Mr. and Mrs. Frederick Pease. Mrs. Pease used to go to bed and lie on a puffy mattress to keep her safe from lightning. Once, it was said, she called out to her husband, "Come and see God's fireworks!" and thereupon a great flash came out of the sky and she was blind ever after.

Grace Allen had two older brothers, but I am sure it was she who brought the fresh color, sparkle, and action to Starbuck's Neck and the old town at large. At first she had a rowboat named *Grace*, then a catboat built for her by Manuel Swartz in his shop at the foot of Daggett Street. Captain Manuel DeLoura named it for her — *Gariota* — which is Portuguese for sea gull.

Grace sailed and swam in a summer life full of holiday brightness. She collected periwinkles from the rocks under the lighthouse bridge and used them for bait with which to catch cunners with hook and line from the steamboat wharf. The cunners she fed to the Allen cats. When the cats had kittens, Mrs. Allen sold them for the benefit of the newly projected St. Andrew's Episcopal Church.

One kitten was sold to a yacht anchored off the lighthouse, and Grace started to swim out to the yacht for a final good-by, but the yacht got under way just as she was about to call out to ask if she could climb aboard. Instead of turning back, she decided to swim on across the harbor to Chappaquiddick, though this was far from being the narrowest part. She swam and swam, and the Chappaquiddick shore continued to lie distantly ahead, so she decided to recite one of her favorite poems, "The Walrus and the Carpenter," before she looked again. Still distant. Again she recited to herself, and so on, until finally, having met the challenge in this way, she reached the sandy shore she had been aiming for. I suppose she was rowed back from the Point by Charlie Osborn, who operated a boat bazaar at the foot of Morse Street.

When a drive to Cottage City was in prospect, Grace was allowed to go to Chester Pease's livery stable and say, "Pansy and the Goddard buggy, please." The Allens were fond of Pansy and her steady gait, and Grace took the reins during the six-mile drive. Pansy would occasionally clamp her beautiful long tail firmly against the reins until Grace managed to pull it up. At Cottage City the rewards were saltwater taffy, popcorn, and rides on the Flying Horses.

Grace liked to call on Tom and Hiram Dunham, two old men who lived in a boathouse near the steamboat

wharf. She remembered them as having "a sort of seafaring gaiety." They owned a double-ender named *We're
Here* in which the two old men liked to cruise around the
harbor and bay. Tom looked like a sailor and Hiram definitely not. But Hiram wore a broad-brimmed black felt
hat identified with the Grand Army of the Republic, in
whose roster he had earned a place. When he met General
Allen on the street one day, he saluted properly, and the
two, as military comrades, exchanged appropriate remarks.

Grace was also a friend of Blind Dan, the town crier and
courier who carried a long staff, as bent and crooked as the
branch of a tree, which it had certainly been. Blind Dan
always called at Sea Rest on Grace's birthday, and Mrs.
Allen would have a basket of good things for him, including a slice of birthday cake. Unseeing, he would turn and
face the voice that came to him. Once, leaving Sea Rest, he
lost himself in shrubbery beside the front gate while
Grace, too embarrassed to go to the rescue, watched him.
But she used to pay calls on him at his small house across
from the cemetery.

At Sea Rest there were two ship's hogsheads out beside
the shed, kept for a water supply with which to irrigate the
garden. Once Grace climbed from one of the hogsheads to
the shed roof. She just happened to have a ripe tomato in
her hand, and when she saw the Reverend William Cleveland Hicks coming in at the front gate, she took a long
swing and creamed him with it nicely.

✧

All this was long ago, and one day word got around that
the talk of a summer hotel was going to amount to something after all. Those who plotted against the primal se-

renity of Starbuck's Neck were Dr. Thomas J. Walker, family physician, and his friend Reverend Luther T. Townsend, a summer visitor from Watertown. Between them they had laid out on paper a development of the open acreage, lots arranged checkerboard fashion along two parallel roads, Raymond Avenue and Prospect Avenue. But the wind shifted and the friends put their money into construction of the Harbor View Hotel, along with funds raised by selling stock.

A contest to select the name of the hotel was run in the *Vineyard Gazette*. Some proposed christenings were pretty fancy, such as "Belvedere," "Magnolia," "Montezuma," "Pilgrim Hall," "Ocean Zephyr," and so on, and someone suggested "The Swasey," in memory of Captain Joseph and his place in Starbuck's Neck history. Dr. Walker wanted "Harbor View" and could have had it without any argument, but in deference to the democratic process he bought up enough ballots for a substantial margin of victory.

The new hotel appeared massive as against the ordinary houses of North Water Street, but within a few years an addition, almost a twin structure, was built in an attempt to attract more business. The overall architecture was probably closest to that earlier called American Carpenter's Renaissance, but Victorian would do as well, with justice to the high-rising and sharply pointed gables and rampant bay windows.

A difficulty not unseen but countered with hope and wishful arithmetic was that the "heated term," as journalists then liked to call it, lasted no more than ten or twelve weeks, a short time in which to earn interest on the investment and pay recurring bills. After Labor Day the battens were put on the windows, and northeasters began to flood the verandas with rain and not too much later to heap them with snow or sleet.

Some stockholders were wiped out, but Dr. Walker and Reverend Townsend held on. Then, after two or three years, with the new rooms added to the summer capacity, business began to improve. The hotel, nevertheless, was offered for sale under the terms of the mortgage, and the doctor and the minister bid it in, Dr. Walker later acquiring the whole property. At last, the costs of construction and the usual extras having been paid up, the Harbor View became exactly what had been intended, the seminal nucleus of a colony of summer visitors increasing with generations.

The Allens had watched the hotel take shape and listened to the sounds of hammer and saw with misgivings. They even went so far as to buy land elsewhere, with a water view, though not so fine as that at Starbuck's Neck, for purposes of retreat. In the end, though, they stayed on.

When one of the John Wesley Pease cats, a tortoiseshell matron named Calico, retired under the Harbor View to have kittens, Grace crawled from the Allen side of the privet hedge through a gap in the foundation and brought the cat family out. John Wesley now referred to the cat as Harley, and Aunt Lucy said, "You know what that stands for, Gracie?" and then explained in a whisper behind her hand, "Harlot — isn't that awful?"

A block away on North Water Street and across Cottage Street at the corner, the Charity Norton house was now rented for the summer by the Marshall Shepard family from New Jersey. The Shepards had also joined the summer colony, in a manner of speaking, through marriage,

since young Marshall Shepard's grandfather, Calvin, had married an Edgartown girl for his second wife. Charity, by whose name the house was known, was the wife of Captain John Oliver Norton and had sailed on all his whaling voyages with him. If she hadn't, it was said he would not have come home alive.

Theodore S. Wimpenney, grandson of Captain Robert, had signed on in his youth as a preventer boatsteerer with Captain Norton on the "Ionia." Theodore, whom I knew well when he was an old man, told me that a wholesale desertion from the ship was planned at Quiriquina Island, opposite the town of Talcahuano, Chile. Captain Norton had twelve of the supposed deserters lashed in the rigging when Charity happened on deck and asked John what that was for.

"I'm going to have 'em thrashed," said John.

"Oh no, you're not," said Charity, and he didn't.

I should have asked how the captain saved face, if he did, but Theodore seemed to feel the point had been made, and I thought so at the time.

There were other incidents of the kind, and I thought of amending Longfellow's line to read, "The wind's will is a woman's will," as it often was, even at sea, in the old days.

Young Marshall Shepard walked out one morning along North Water Street, which was surfaced then with crushed scallop shells, bleached white, as far as the Harbor View, and at the end of the street he watched with astonishment the great waterspouts of 1896, a short distance off Cape Pogue. Towering blackly into a black sky, they remained long enough to be photographed for pictures that would appear in encyclopedias and textbooks. Marshall raced to a

boathouse on the harbor front where several elders of seafaring character sat smoking, spitting, and occasionally
uttering a word or so.

"Waterspout! Waterspout!" yelled the boy, pointing.

Not one of the group paid attention. Marshall ran off
again. The old men were still sitting there when salt water
fell as rain.

Such indifference did not extend to summer people. One
visitor more or less immortalized the event:

> Turn out, turn out, a waterspout
> Is churning up the Bay.
> Turn out, turn out, a waterspout
> Is ours to see today.

◇

Grace Allen was not well acquainted with the Gabrielsons,
though she could remember liking them as neighbors. One
who did remember them well was Captain Antone King
Silva, who used to walk down Main Street followed by his
dog Joe. Joe, mostly setter, was chocolate brown, and held
his tail straight out. "Tony King," as his friends knew him,
and I was one, had been a deep-sea fisherman until his
boat was lost and now sailed and fished in a catboat in
coastal waters. Of Captain Gabrielson he said to me, "He
used to have a Jap boy with him on the *Gallatin*." The
Gallatin was a revenue cutter then based at Edgartown,
commanded by Eric Gabrielson.

So many ironies come down in our annals — the "Jap
boy" on the *Gallatin* and often quartered at the Gabrielson
house — was Charles J. Soong, born on Hainan Island in
the China Sea off the southern coast of Kwangtung Province. Island, town, and strait had been part of China since

the second century B.C., and Charles Soong, when he shipped on the *Gallatin* at Boston, already carried in his young person much of the destiny of the great Chinese subcontinent. Most of us tend to believe in destiny. Some don't.

Isabelle Wimpenney, of my own generation, showed me a picture of Soong at sixteen, a boy who, the more he was trying to appear serious and grown-up, the more he appeared his own grave, youthful, and aspiring presence. Written on the photograph were these words: "Charles J. Soong, presented to his little friend, Harrie L. Wimpenney. Think of me when you play side yard." Harry L. Wimpenney, Isabelle's father, was another grandson of Captain Robert.

Charles J. Soong went back to China. One of his daughters, Mei-ling, who attended a Girl Scout camp on Martha's Vineyard while at an American college, married the generalissimo, Chiang Kai-shek, and became a world leader in her own right. Her sister, Ai-ling, became the bride of H. H. Kung, in direct line from Confucius, whose statesmanship as Chinese minister of finance gave him high world fame. The other sister, Ching-ling, married Sun Yat-sen, founder of the Chinese Republic. There were three brothers. T. V. Soong founded the National Bank of China and later served as foreign minister of China. T. L. Soong became Chinese finance commissioner and a director of the World Bank. T. A. Soong, youngest son of Charles J. Soong, served as collector of internal revenue in China and in other governmental posts. As the matter stands in history, the famous Soong dynasty was domiciled for a time on North Water Street in Edgartown. It may be that some future ambassador from China will dedicate a suitable marker on the house or on the white fence at Starbuck's Neck.

The premises themselves are not undeserving. A biographer of Captain Gabrielson wrote: "He set up his home in a house of moderate but dignified appearance. Edgartown mariners lived among surroundings of restrained luxury, not in homes of passing comfort but in stately houses whose simple, modified classical architecture was an expression of the New England temperament. In sound orthodoxy the 27-year-old Gabrielson acquired an imposing house at the time of his marriage, a house befitting the niece of Judge Pease, the town's squire."

I have gone to the West Side cemetery to visit the burial lot of the Gabrielsons, thinking all the time of young Charles Soong and his little friend, Harry Wimpenney. A massive block of pink-gray marble stands in the center of the lot, which is curbed with granite. A single name, Gabrielson, stands out in large letters on the marble. Beside it on the right a granite marker is inscribed, "Eric Gabrielson, born Stavanger, Norway — July 18, 1840– April 10, 1901." On the left is an identical marker with the information "Mary Belle Wimpenney, His Wife, April 3, 1849–Oct. 8, 1901."

These names complete a coalition I should like to invoke in proceedings for the defense of Starbuck's Neck against the plans of the Harbor View Hotel corporation, abetted by the Commonwealth of Massachusetts.

⌒

This morning I woke Graham at 4:30, thinking it was 5:30. There really is quite a difference, and you notice it more after you're up. A crescent moon hung low, and as we walked along the lighthouse causeway I thought it should get out of the way to give a clear field, or sky, to the expected rising of the sun. Not that there could be a collision, but I didn't want our spectacles mixed. The air was bitterly cold and so clear that the stars were keenly bright.

How often have Graham and I watched for the sun to appear above Chappaquiddick, and how often have I searched for words with which to express the poetry of sunrise. In high school my teacher praised the *Odyssey* for its often-repeated metaphor, "When the rosy-fingered dawn appeared." But in all my watching sunrises I have never seen any fingers in the eastern sky — layers, patches, streaks, and singular creatures, but never fingers, and of all the morning hues "rose" seems to me the rarest.

The *Odyssey* persists in my mind also for that other unfortunate figure, "They smote the foaming water with their oars." A clumsy attempt at locomotion, surely, and how odd for a seafaring race not to feather its oars even in childhood, by instinct, if not by instruction, in the way long known to the generations of Martha's Vineyard.

The "break" of day sounds like a celestial fracturing, as I suppose it is, though without violence or noise. Sunrise breaks and night falls, and the integrity of the world is not disturbed.

The lowland under the bank across from the Harbor View and North Water Street is awakened to color at any time of year as the sunlight reaches over and into it. In late fall and winter the colors are those of a tapestry, but even more of a sampler of eloquent but subdued mood. Beach grass of different degrees of tan, cinnamon (here the scent of spice comes in), sorrel, russet, maroon; thickets of bayberry, black and twiggy in winter, the fuzzy remains of many kinds of goldenrod, lichens and mosses, stunted oak, and wild cherry. All good, homely colors expressive of texture as well.

North Water Street, black-topped and impervious to old uses and customs, is no longer the unpretentious thoroughfare kept white and respectable, as well as useful, through the use of crushed and bleached scallop shells. The change was wrought in the WPA days of the Great Depression, no one then imagining the present incessant summer traffic of buses and automobiles. What you didn't know didn't hurt you.

The innocence of the year 1913 is conveyed to the modern understanding in a letter of that year written by an observer: "Mrs. Dinsmore was in the Thayer Cottage. My first view of her was walking down the middle of North Water Street from the direction of the Harbor View, looking perfectly adorable in a pale blue gown, white gloves, and a parasol over her head. She was laughing and talking to an escort on either side, a picture to be remembered."

It wouldn't have been remembered but for the chance emergence of this old letter; and, not remembered, it could hardly have been imagined in this new generation. I am one of the few now living who saw the fourteen-foot hollyhock Mrs. Dinsmore grew in her North Water Street garden years ago. If people grow hollyhocks now they are likely to incline toward the new hybridized double ones, which are different flowers entirely and a retreat from the culture of my youth.

At least an equally disturbing enterprise is that of a different sort, the filling in of the Starbuck's Neck wetland for construction of two houses and a tennis court. This is the Age of Strangers.

Lines come to me from a sonnet Grace Allen wrote after she had lived a good while into the present century and its alienations.

> The days are like a garment that we wear
> Too oft indifferently, oft self-betrayed,
> Forgetting that the weaving years are made
> Of our long memories. Take then a share
> In the blue brightness of a summer hour
> In the soft whiteness of a sandy shore.

OUR LAWYER SAID that I should telephone Mr. Sullivan so that I would be sure of meeting him at Starbuck's Neck. Mr. Sullivan's card read, "DEQE, Land and Water Use, Southeastern Regional Office." The "DEQE" stands for "Department of Environmental Quality Engineering."

Mr. Sullivan said over the telephone, "The only reason I'm coming down is so that if I'm asked I can say that I have seen the site." The site is the wet lowland under the bank opposite and below the Harbor View, shelving off to beach and lagoon. The site is also referred to as "the locus."

The bank above it is perhaps eighteen feet higher than mean low water, falling away into a smother of wild growth to the now disputed marshy wetland. Even Mr.

Sullivan said this was all wetland. Next to Lane Lovell's house, which on one side borders the walk to the lighthouse causeway, is a pool where ducks often swim. Its water, deeper blue than that of lagoon and harbor, reflects the sun jointly with them in a harmony of nature. In late July and early August a margin of steeplebush rises with spires of pink blossoms, showing where fresh water seeps into the pond to meet an infiltration of salt.

Squarely in this pool or pond is where the Harbor View corporation has applied for permission to build one of its two projected houses. Our town Conservation Commission held a hearing and used its limited authority, though maybe its authority was not so limited as it believed, to protect the pool from being filled. There is an argument as to whether town conservation commissions in Massachusetts can deny applications or only impose conditions. In any case, the course of expediency is not to vote an outright denial and risk an appeal to the courts.

So, except for the pool where ducks often swim, the corporation's application was generally approved. The corporation appealed to upset the restriction, and we appealed because the restriction was not broader. "We" are fourteen residents of Edgartown, the list headed by myself, Lane Lovell, and Mary Wakeman, who lives in the old Wimpenney house. The others usually come under the heading of "et al." The two appeals were what brought Mr. Sullivan to the site so that he could say he had seen it in case anyone should ask him.

Getting out of the car, he remarked, "It's all wetland," and I mistook this for encouragement. We walked to the level of the marsh — Mr. Sullivan; Ed Tyra, chairman of the town Conservation Commission; Lane Lovell; young

Jeff Norton, lawyer for the hotel corporation; Dean Swift, surveyor and engineer, who spread out the plans filed by the hotel; and myself. Mr. Sullivan then shared with us what he called "hypothetical thinking," the burden of which proved to be that none of the seven concerns of the DEQE seemed to be involved here.

Jurisdiction of the DEQE is defined in Chapter 131, Section 40, of the General Laws, the so-called Wetlands Protection Act, its scope limited to: effect on public or private water supply, ground water supply, flood control, storm-damage protection, prevention of pollution, protection of land containing shellfish, protection of fisheries — all severely practical matters. Pollution under the act meant sewage or chemical poisons, of course, but not that sort of contamination by civilized living that pushes back the frontiers of wildlife and claims more territory from nature.

"Are you concerned with ecology?" I asked.

"No," said Mr. Sullivan.

It looked to him, he said, as if 131-40 — the almost affectionate phrase used officially to identify the Wetlands Protection Act — mandated the filling of this wetland, pond and all, as applied for by the Harbor View. I thought this an astonishing reversal, and so it was, to a layman, since the act was being turned into an instrument for the extinguishing of wetlands.

I asked Mr. Sullivan, "Are you familiar with the order of the Martha's Vineyard Commission?"

"Have you got a copy?" he asked.

I gave him one. The Martha's Vineyard Commission was established in 1974 under an innovative land-use act sponsored by the Republican conservationist governor, Francis W. Sargent, often known as "Sarge" or Frank. I had known him so at times.

In order to understand the commission and how it was brought about, one must first be informed about the Islands Trust Bill, usually known as the Kennedy Bill, and I will go into that presently.

Under the authority of the Sargent Act, the commission had designated the coastal rim of Martha's Vineyard as a District of Critical Planning Concern, separating it into an inland zone and a shore zone, the latter defined as "land from mean low water to 100 feet inland of the inland edge of any beach or marsh grasses, and 100 feet inland of the crest of any bluff exceeding a height of 15 feet." By this definition our wetland fell within the shore zone, subject to regulations prohibiting alterations or construction of any kind except certain nonresidential structures allowable under special permit. At a hearing before the commission we had presented as an expert witness Dr. John Teal, coauthor, with his wife, of the book *Life and Death of a Salt Marsh*.

"I went down to the property this evening," Dr. Teal testified. "My feet are still wet." I had gone with him, and my feet were still wet, too. He had found marsh and dune grasses, particularly *Spartina patens*, growing in abundance and satisfying the commission's definition that put "all this area within the shore zone."

The commission then determined, under an authority much broader and more comprehensive than that of the DEQE, that development along the shore and in the wetlands would be "detrimental to the public welfare and cause irreversible damage to the land and waters of Edgartown and Martha's Vineyard." In this fragile area, the order went on, development would "increase the possibility of pollution by the destruction of wetlands and create hazards to the future residents of the proposed development." Information submitted to the commission had shown that the area "is subject to hurricane surge floods and contains wetland vegetation. Finding no benefits to offset these detrimental impacts, the Commission therefore disallows approval of such application by the Town of Edgartown and Town Clerk."

The commission had also noted the visual quality of the region, including the wild bank that the hotel intended to secure with interlocking railroad ties.

I have no way of knowing whether Mr. Sullivan looked at the commission's order on his way downtown, but presumably he did not, since he stopped at Main Street to inform the town Conservation Commission through its secretary that he was issuing a superseding order removing the restriction imposed by the commission and allowing the application of the Harbor View in toto: house in the duck pond, railroad ties woven into the bank, another house beyond, and tennis court between, and the wetland gone forever.

~

The first time I met Edward M. Kennedy must have been back in 1952 when his older brother, John F. Kennedy, was running for senator against Henry Cabot Lodge. I think Bob Carroll was chairman of the Democratic town committee, as his father had been before him. In the context of Edgartown affairs and friendships — and also of politics — it would be strained and unnatural to speak of Robert J. Carroll otherwise than as "Bob."

The town Democrats had invited John F. Kennedy to visit Martha's Vineyard for a round of campaigning, the kind of tour that gives a candidate a chance to "meet people" in a range from the mothers of babies to influential elder citizens. It was in the nature of a hotly contested senatorial race that John F. Kennedy could not take time from the major circuits, and that his younger brother should represent him.

I happened to be coming along from the direction of Main Street when Bob Carroll and Ted Kennedy stepped out the front door of the Coffee Shop. Of course Bob introduced me, and I had an interesting, but too scanty, impression of the younger brother. He was attractively young, and also attractive apart from the one element of youth. He wore an overcoat against the raw, glum weather, and I do not remember that he said much. I didn't have anything in particular to say, either.

Bob was Edgartown-born, apt in school, and had served in World War II from 1943 until 1945 with the Seabees and in the Pacific theater. He ran for selectman of Edgartown in 1958 and was remarkably elected by a single vote. In a succession of three-year terms he won re-election by 4 votes, and then by 106 votes, a measure of political progress not too common in town affairs.

In 1964 he was a candidate for state representative on the Democratic ticket against a popular Republican veteran of many years' service, emerging as a loser but with the strong total of 1156 against 2057 for the entrenched veteran. It seemed obvious that Bob Carroll had made a political mark and represented a considerable popularity and political skill. He had dealt successfully in real estate and engaged in the restaurant business, and in 1965, together with a former state senator, Allen M. Jones, he bought the Harbor View Hotel and became its managing owner.

Meantime, an advertisement he had placed in the *Vine-*

yard Gazette during his campaign for representative seemed a statement that, looked at a few years later, might have been taken for a precursor of the Kennedy Bill:

> These are important years, indeed, for Martha's Vineyard and for the way of life it has managed to maintain, quite often in the face of great odds. All of us who love the Island see its way of life threatened constantly, not only by problems that arise within the community but also from those that arise from without.
>
> We all know that the Vineyard is unique and we want to keep her that way, a difficult task as the Island is "discovered" by more and more people. I believe that the Vineyard is bound to grow, but the danger is that she will grow in an undisciplined and eventually ruinous manner. An orderly, sensible growth will require strength of leadership not only on just the town level, but also on the county and state levels. The Vineyard's leaders should be people who are not only aware of her problems, but also willing and able to fight for constructive solutions.

The origin of the Kennedy Bill can be traced back over a long period, and one generating event occurred in this same year, 1964. John B. Oakes of the *New York Times*, a dedicated and expert conservationist and equally a dedicated lover of Martha's Vineyard, arranged with the National Park Service for an inspection of the Island. It seemed natural that the success of the Cape Cod National Seashore should suggest a study of any possible adaptation of its experience to the interests of conservation on Martha's Vineyard.

John M. Kauffmann, special assistant to the director of the park service, made a report of this inspection trip, on which he was accompanied by Mr. Oakes and by Mr. and Mrs. Richard M. Pough. Mr. Kauffmann referred to the growing concern felt by Mr. Oakes over "the erosion of the

Island's scenic features as development creeps over the landscape. The blight of unbridled subdivision and the inroads of tasteless commercial exploitation are only just beginning on Martha's Vineyard, but as an alert and sensitive conservationist, Mr. Oakes sees the handwriting on the wall. So, of course, does Mr. Pough, a professional conservationist long engaged in battling to protect natural areas. And so does Henry Hough, the local newspaper editor."

Of particular concern, Mr. Kauffmann went on, "is the fact that the Island is absolutely unprotected against exploitation. It is without zoning of any kind (with the exception of two or three neighborhood associations), and the local population will have none of it. Moreover, the Island's nonresident owners, who own perhaps 85 percent of the Island, have no voice in the Island's government."

A little later in the report came this passage: "What to do about Martha's Vineyard was the question we discussed over and over again all weekend. In a sense, of course, Martha's Vineyard is simply a classic example of a problem which is becoming apparent all over the nation and which can be particularly virulent in New England, where few of the beautiful old villages and traditional landscapes have any protection."

Mr. Kauffmann urged continuing interest in the Island on the part of the park service, and concluded, "Conservation on Martha's Vineyard calls for the kind of innovation and ingenuity that has marked Secretary Udall's conservation successes. If we can find the right avenues for action, we can do much to preserve the kind of environment on Martha's Vineyard and many other places that is symbolic of the American scene at its best."

A lapse of years, and in 1969 the Dukes County Plan-

ning and Economic Development Commission, funded by
federal grant and looking toward a comprehensive plan
for the county, contracted for a study by the Boston engineering firm of Metcalf and Eddy. Two years later, in its
report, the engineering firm wrote: "The County, one of
the few bastions of rural environmental splendor left along
the coastline of the United States, faces clear and present
danger from despoilers."

When the Island would contract "environmental terminal cancer" could not be predicted, the report said, but
the next five years would be critical: "If a definite and
well-ordered program of preventive and prescriptive medi-
cine is not undertaken immediately or within the next five
years, by 1975 the Vineyard will undoubtedly have contracted environmental terminal cancer."

The commission had not looked for anything of this sort.
I suppose the operative interest, apart from federal funding, which is always attractive, could be defined in the
words of the commission's title, "economic development."
So the Metcalf and Eddy report was received with disap-
pointment and resentment. Part of it was suppressed, the
rest of it ignored, and the censored text published so that
further federal funding could be obtained.

The commission undertook another study within its
chosen bounds that would be as solid and safe as most such
studies and reports. Meantime, three Island towns had
adopted zoning codes, a forward step but far from what
Metcalf and Eddy meant by a well-ordered program.

In 1971, also, Senator Kennedy introduced a bill au-
thorizing an Interior Department study of the feasibility
of including the Nantucket Sound Islands within the Cape
Cod National Seashore. No one was enthusiastic about

this, and neither in the long run was Senator Kennedy, who concluded that there was no need for another in the long series of federal, state, and local studies of the Islands.

I think it must have been in late August or early September of 1971 when Lochinvar, Graham's collie predecessor, and I, who had been out much later than usual, arrived home a little past midnight and heard the telephone ringing. I remember the warmth and sweetness of the summer night, the Milky Way overhead, the invitation of time itself, which seemed to be standing still.

I answered the telephone, and it was Rose Styron asking if I would speak with Senator Kennedy. He had sailed over from Cape Cod, I think with a party of young people, and I could imagine the scene on the broad Styron lawn that extended to the harbor shore.

Ted Kennedy took the telephone and spoke of his concern for the future of the Vineyard and Nantucket, two islands that would be overwhelmed if some protection could not be found for their unique resources and character. He thought there must be some workable concept, perhaps adapted from Old World experience. Then he said, "I'd be willing to stand considerable heat to do it." Words of summer that made the best seem possible, and forthright realism too. "Considerable heat" — how high a price? But worth paying.

In April 1972 Senator Kennedy introduced the Islands Trust Bill, embodying not only his concern but a working plan. The Islands, he said, "combine an unusual history, a fragile ecology, a natural beauty, and other values unmatched on the east coast of the United States. These Islands have, until recently, escaped the intense second home and suburbanized development pressures which are so characteristic of much of the rest of the coastline of the United States.

"In the past four years, however, the Nantucket Sound Islands have become the target of the same kind of pressures which have irretrievably destroyed large parts of our natural heritage. This type of development scatters houses haphazardly across the rolling moors; sits them down on fragile dunes and in coastal marshes without regard for delicate, natural balances; drives up local taxes to pay for the increased demand for municipal services; and with an irreversible finality changes what was once a wild and beautiful landscape into one indistinguishable from big city suburbs."

The Islands Trust Bill, he said, was "a working document," with changes to be developed in discussions and meetings with Island residents and others. Any sort of federal preserve was to be avoided, since it would ignore the fragility of the Islands, chill their liveliness and, in fact, accelerate their destruction.

A trust proposed by the bill would be administered as to policy by a commission of twenty-one members, eighteen from the Islands, "working in partnership with the Secretary of the Interior." There would be four classes of trust lands: Forever Wild, including the beaches, which would become public domain, with any existing buildings to be removed after twenty-one years; Scenic Preservation; County Control; and Town Control. An early amendment allowed controlled building in Scenic Preservation areas, and another merged the county and town categories. It was emphasized that the process of discussion and amendment was to continue.

Senator Kennedy found a direct precedent for the bill in

a 1970 Interior Department report analyzing the Island trust concept and its application, and also in land use and environmental legislation in several states. The bill also drew on existing federal law. But it was still innovative and imaginative.

The first airing of the bill on Martha's Vineyard was at a press conference called by Thomas Hale in the office of his shipyard. He was not an elected official, but the crisis of the Islands had concerned him and his wife, both of them grounded in principles of land planning. K. Dun Gifford, a former aide of Senator Kennedy and a Nantucket seasonal resident, had asked the Hales for help in the groundwork for the bill.

The "elected officials," a phrase they were to emphasize over and over again, were outraged that they had been ignored up to now, and the press conference was held in a darkening mood. The day had not passed before there were threats to burn down Tom Hale's shipyard, and when a respected citizen deplored such threats, another respected citizen snapped out, "Well, it ought to be burned down."

There was no doubt whatever that the local power structures of Martha's Vineyard and Nantucket had been deliberately by-passed in the preparation of a draft — a working document — in which not only the elected officials but representatives of all shades of independent opinion on the Islands should be involved.

Presently Dun Gifford, sized up by more than one observer as a "Kennedy type," came to the Vineyard to explain the bill and to solicit questions and comments. Dun, youthful, keen, and good-looking, was also an informed and thoughtful political intellectual. Scotty Reston characterized him accurately as a "pro." In my own experience I have learned how important "pros" are, because there is much truth in the old saying that God Almighty hates an amateur.

In the chilly gloom of the Harborside Bar and Grill at Edgartown, not yet fairly out of its winter lay-up, Dun faced an audience of "elected officials" and some others.

"Who drafted this bill?" was the immediate and then often-repeated question.

"Senator Kennedy drafted it."

Someone yelled, "Withdraw the bill!" and the cry was repeated.

"Senator Kennedy will not withdraw the bill."

Bob Carroll stood a little way back, not at the rear, matching Dun's coolness and self-possession. He was the old Kennedy friend and ally who had been ignored. It was understood that the friendship formed in 1952 had continued, and on occasion Senator Kennedy had flown from the Island in Bob Carroll's plane. It may well have been that he felt he had been slapped in the face, but he was giving no sign of ill temper or resentment.

The bill, Bob said at this meeting with Dun Gifford, "is the work of a few people who think they are intellectually and socially superior." The senator was acting as judge and jury, and democratic processes in the county would be suspended if the bill were passed. "You are trying to impose something on us . . . You can't buy these Islands for $20 million" — this being the initial appropriation proposed in the bill.

"We have no idea of buying the Islands."

"Land that can't be built on is worthless. This is like the dictatorship in Greece."

"They shoot people over there," Dun said.

"That's the only thing you haven't put in the bill."

One selectman had counted only five references in the bill to the administering commission, as against forty-four references to the secretary of the interior. It was declared that this proved an intent of "federal control" of the Islands.

In the evening, Dun met a packed audience of the general public, which distilled as much vehemence or more. But the first test by ballot showed forty percent favoring the bill at this early stage, and the town of Tisbury refused by majority vote at town meeting to direct its board of selectmen to oppose the bill in the name of the town.

A joint Islands Action Committee for Nantucket and Martha's Vineyard, with Bob Carroll as chairman for the Vineyard, was organized to fight the bill. "Don't Trust the Trust" and "Island Trust for the Upper Crust" said the bumper stickers. The wife of a Chilmark selectman wrote a letter opposing the bill, concluding with the words, "Through our own efforts and with God's help we will be able to preserve and conserve our own Islands."

But Ginny Jones, granddaughter of Joe Howes, native patriarch of West Tisbury, wrote in advocacy of the bill, using the refrain "We can do it ourselves!" with irony.

We can do it ourselves.

Land sales and prices are booming. Islanders can hardly resist selling. The Registry of Deeds used to fill a book a decade; now it's a book full of transactions every five or six weeks.

We can do it ourselves.

Roads are appearing all over the scene . . . with ticky-tacky little split-level dream houses. Small-lot developments proliferate endlessly.

We can do it ourselves.

Parking is almost nonexistent . . . The ferries run
shuttle schedules . . . The boats run hours late; tempers
are frayed and manners and patience nil.
We can do it ourselves.

And so on. Some other important early voices were
raised in support. Dr. Nicholas Freydberg, retired psy-
chologist living all year at Chilmark, characterized the
bill as "just about our last chance" and held a discussion
meeting at his house, joined in the late evening by Dun
Gifford. For this Dr. Freydberg was attacked by the full
board of the Chilmark selectmen as a Johnny-come-lately
and a do-gooder. A neighbor refused to let him walk across
her land to the beach. Out of this meeting, however, came
a committee, mostly native and all-year in membership, to
support the bill, with amendments.

Addressing the Martha's Vineyard Lions Club, Bob Carroll attacked the bill as "a complete lie." He said, "We
have the loveliest community in the world right here on
Martha's Vineyard and you and I have made it that way
without any outside help." After a while Dun Gifford came
again to explain proposed amendments to the Island selectmen, and the meeting bogged him down with questions
and digressions. Just before midnight Bob Carroll was re-
calling a talk with Roger N. Baldwin some years previously.

"He was worried about our having town meetings when
all the bright people weren't around here. The other day I
went to Scarsdale where all the geniuses came from and I
saw how they've screwed up Scarsdale. I don't want that
for Edgartown."

That the bill represented a cleavage between summer
people and all-year Islanders was taken up mostly by visiting reporters, who had decided in advance that it must be

so. But as to the polarization of the two sides, opponents and proponents, there could be no doubt. The relatively small part played by logic might have been astonishing to anyone unfamiliar with politics and, seen in small compass on so clear an issue, perhaps astonishing even to the politically sophisticated.

Dun Gifford again assessed the range of local choices: zoning, subdivision control, health code, building code, historic district commission — "Even if all the towns had in force and effect each of these land tools; and even if each of these tools was aggressively enforced to the fullest extent possible under state and local laws and the home rule amendment — the net effect would be not to limit the number and extent of subdivisions, but to control their design, placement, and appearance." He added that in perspective it could be said that the Kennedy Bill would create and restore local control where it did not today exist. If this statement was arguable, no one attempted to argue it — and the quest for an "alternative" went on.

It seemed to have been found in a state bill sponsored by Governor Sargent, who believed that there should be both a federal and state role in "the common goal of protecting these Islands." On one Island visit Governor Sargent said, "There is not one inch of available land on the Island that is not being eyed by developers today." A revised Islands Trust Bill was designed to be compatible with the Sargent Bill.

In July 1973 the Senate Subcommittee on Parks and Recreation held a hearing on the amended Kennedy Bill in the gymnasium of the Tisbury school. Bob Carroll was one of the many who spoke. I was one also, on the other side.

Bob identified himself as a lifelong Edgartown resident and businessman, a former selectman, president of the Martha's Vineyard Chamber of Commerce, and cochairman of the Islands Action Committee. He quoted the definition of a trusteeship — "the condition of being confided to another's care or guard."

"For such drastic action to become necessary," he went on, "there should be some evidence that the victim is incompetent or deserves to be punished for crimes against the state, or sime similar offense. This is bewildering, because the crime apparently has been in preserving and conserving our resources far better than other areas in the United States. The penalties for this crime seem to be the loss of effective town government and demotion to the status of second-class citizens, eventually to be retrained as berry-pickers or janitors for a favored few . . .

"In April 1972, when the bill was introduced, I happened to be reading *Bury My Heart at Wounded Knee*. The concept of 'manifest destiny,' so prevalent through the book, seems to me to sum up the results of the trust bill if passed . . .

"Senator Kennedy explained to his colleagues on May 31, 1973, 'The bill could establish a mechanism by which access to the Island by water or air can be controlled. If access were to be unlimited, then the very purpose of this bill, preservation and conservation, would be thwarted.' I question any group's legal authority to limit access to the Island. Such action suggests a whole new country where small groups decide who is to go where, when and by what method. It becomes apparent that the real intent of the bill is to impose ten-acre zoning, prevent us from going to our own beaches, and generally usurping our rights as citizens of the United States . . ."

Then Bob referred to a desirable "stiffening of our laws concerning land use by the state and local governments — which, incidentally, is the way I think this can be accomplished."

The chosen weapon of the opposition to the Kennedy Bill, the "alternative" of a state bill, was supported in a telegram from the junior senator from Massachusetts, Edward W. Brooke. The telegram, read to the meeting, asked that consideration of the Islands Trust Bill be deferred while the Islanders, with the assistance of Governor Sargent's land use bill for the Vineyard, "solved the problem for themselves."

At one point Bob Carroll, speaking vigorously, demanded to know why Senator Kennedy had gone ahead with redrafting his proposed legislation after promising not to "cram anything down the throats of the Islanders." Senator Kennedy broke in to say, "I'm not going to permit my view to be distorted and misrepresented."

The hearing lasted long into the afternoon, and as the day faded into a warm summer twilight, I met Senator Kennedy for the second time, on the Styron lawn, that green expanse on the harborside of Vineyard Haven. Senator Bible, chairman of the subcommittee, was there, and a gathering of Islanders who for the most part supported the bill. The air again was sweet and softened into a remembered July languor while the world seemed to rest and all things to become possible. I thought of Senator Kennedy's telephone call from the Styron house, and how he had said, "I'd be willing to stand considerable heat to do it."

Governor Sargent came to the Island for a hearing on his bill, held by a state legislative committee. Among those who attended was Edward J. Logue, former head of the Boston Redevelopment Authority, a sojourner in Chilmark and a member of a conservation group, the Vineyard Open Land Foundation, which he had helped to organize. Douglas Cabral's report in the *Vineyard Gazette* said that Mr. Logue came to the hearing "Bermuda-shorted and relaxed, to present a section-by-section critique of the bill, which in his view offered 'limited powers and meagre resources to pursue fuzzy objectives.' "

Anne W. Simon, author of the book *No Island Is an Island*, which was directed to the problem of Martha's Vineyard, told the committee: "In my opinion the bill as it stands takes a critical land-planning step backwards. It is a proposal for the total development of Martha's Vineyard, planned development to be sure, but development nevertheless."

Bob Carroll supported the bill but only, as he said, because it offered a way to avoid having Vineyard land use "controlled by Washington."

Mr. Logue presently remarked that the strongest supporters of Governor Sargent's bill were clearly the strongest opponents of Senator Kennedy's bill, and on the other hand the strongest opponents of Governor Sargent's bill were the most-committed partisans of the Kennedy bill. "It's enough," Mr. Logue said, "to make you wonder what the hell is going on down here."

In his own explanation Governor Sargent described his bill as a planning and regulatory measure, not primarily a preservation bill; and his aide suggested an amendment deleting the words "preserve and conserve" from the bill's statement of purposes.

A little later an observer would speak of the "incredible effort expended by numerous people during two years of weekly meetings and in the preparation of fourteen drafts" of the Sargent Bill. The governor's aide said he had learned "the need of patience in dealing with local officials." He said this obviously with strong feeling.

Ultimately a referendum in the six townships of Martha's Vineyard voted 1305 to 694 to endorse the Sargent Bill, and the bill was enacted into law in late spring of 1974. The opponents of the Kennedy Bill could point to an existing "alternative." The Kennedy Bill, now supported both by Senator Brooke and Congressman Gerry Studds, was passed by the Senate but failed of action in the House before time ran out. In Washington, opponents of the bill said they already had a commission and did not need or want any other.

At the final hearing in Vineyard Haven on the Kennedy Bill, Jon Ahlbum, now president of the Martha's Vineyard Chamber of Commerce, told the House subcommittee on national parks and recreation: "We are simply asking that Congress end the effort to put the federal government in charge of our lives." An astonished Congressman Seiberling of Ohio remarked that in his view the Kennedy Bill in no way represented federal intrusion, but it did represent almost a blank check to the local communities and amounted to "an intrusion into the U.S. Treasury."

Having got rid of the Kennedy Bill, it remained for the opponents to get rid of the Sargent legislation as soon as opportunity offered. Meantime, however, the Martha's Vineyard Commission had been established. It was to become legally operative on a Tuesday. On the preceding Friday, filling for tennis courts began in the wetland opposite and below the Harbor View Hotel. This was allowable under action taken by the town Conservation Commission, and an attorney for the hotel corporation assured the selectmen that nothing further would be done until prescribed permits were obtained.

In the succession of events, which pay no attention to irony, Bob Carroll, the most prominent leader of opposition to the Kennedy Bill and supporter of the Sargent Bill as an "alternative," now stood in confrontation, through his managing ownership of the Harbor View, with the new Martha's Vineyard Commission and its regulations applying to the coastal district.

∽

Up to this point, I suppose, our group had spent something on the order of $3000 in the legal steps for protection of the Harbor View wetlands, and had come up against not merely a rejection but a countervailing order and a stronger opponent, the DEQE. We were worse off than when we started because the DEQE was wholly on the side of the Harbor View.

The DEQE had been engaged mainly in the whole or partial destruction of wetlands in different parts of the state, and the law seemed directed to that purpose. The Massachusetts Audubon Society found that "the law has allowed any number of formerly wild swamps and marshes to be turned into housing lots and industrial sites. In many cases the only indication that an area was once a wetland is the presence of some conduit under the site which is designed to carry off the flood waters that once were held in the spongy soils of the former wetland. In fact, more often than not, wetland cases degenerate into arguments over the size of the conduits rather than the real issue, which is the loss of a natural wetland."

A Conservation Law Foundation member observed that

to the DEQE "there is nothing in God's world that cannot be fixed through an engineering solution. Sometimes the engineering approach is the only rational solution to problems, but in many instances it only promotes construction in wetlands."

The view of Dick Pough, who had accompanied John Oakes and the park service man on a Martha's Vineyard inspection tour so long ago, was succinctly stated:

"The earth's most valuable resource is its stock of different species, races, and strains of living organisms, each of which has unique attributes and potentialities. At the very least it has taken nature a billion years to produce these forms of life and bring them to their present state of development, and they can very properly be termed the earth's 'biological elements' . . .

"Some of the biotic communities that are living storehouses for these biological communities are safeguarded, but some are not. Every year sees precious last remnants of once extensive plant-animal communities vanish . . . Only in an organism's natural setting can be determined what the evolutionary forces were that moulded it in its present form."

No one knew much about the biological communities of Starbuck's Neck, though their evolution had proceeded through a vastness of time; but none of this was any concern of the DEQE. No considerations of the sort were admitted under the seven headings of 131-40.

After Mr. Sullivan and the others had gone, Graham and I saw nineteen snowy egrets fly over from Chappaquiddick to feed in the lagoon. The lagoon is a popular resort for egrets, ducks, and heron and for the Canada geese that are numerous in winter, when stress of weather makes them tame. It's an experience to feel a Canada goose tugging at your back pocket for corn.

The Martha's Vineyard Commission went far beyond the DEQE in its standards, considering the appropriateness or inappropriateness of developments and evaluating unique historic values, irreplaceable views, unique cultural resources, recreational opportunities having profound importance to the community and its development, destruction of natural resources, and also factors that might enhance the health, safety, and general welfare of residents and visitors and of future generations. The DEQE does not simply ignore considerations such as these — it opposes them, excludes them, insists that they shall not prevail.

We were warned that as ordinary citizens we should not go before the DEQE without a lawyer, and I am sure this was excellent advice. The warning applies to all hearings before official bodies. It is not our opponents but the administering officials who will make fools of us if they can.

We asked our lawyer, Jerry Healy, to appeal from Mr. Sullivan's superseding order. The last thing we will be allowed to say is that this natural wetland would be best let alone. The modern world wants something done with, or to, anything lying outdoors in aloneness of character.

GRAHAM AND I went out after supper into the evening darkness, so much earlier than it had been. The houses along North Water Street were mostly closed for the winter, and only a few lights glowed from Chappaquiddick across the harbor. Even if it had not been for the unaccustomed darkness, an emptiness would have told us that the summer people had departed. One gets to know that feeling well.

Long ago on Martha's Vineyard when houses were widely separated, or even when they weren't so widely separated any more but most people could remember when they had been, a familiar word at parting when vacationers closed their houses and left for the city, was always, "We'll miss your lights." And as the evenings shortened and bedtime came right after sundown, the neighboring lights of the summer season were missed. Instead of a spot of brightness, a glow beyond the ridge or wood or the turn of the road, a greater and a different darkness had closed in, to become darker and darker through the long winter until June.

The old word in autumn is still spoken by traditional Vineyarders, "We'll miss your lights." Not all modern vacationers have experienced the like of our winter darkness and the sense of custom that prompts such an expression. A mythic quality has been diminished. Miss your lights? What an odd thing to say! You won't miss us, it seems, but only the lights you could see from our windows at night. How come? Would it not be more polite to say you will miss us, our comings and goings, our little politenesses, our greetings day by day?

No, not really. Comings and goings are one thing, and lights at night, the company and assurance of them, the plainest symbol of neighborliness and companionship not too close or too far removed, have a significance apart. What we miss is not something modern but something old. Not personal or impersonal, either, but a special thing, a predestined repetition in the lifetime experience of man.

Argue this as one will, the truth remains. We'll miss your lights.

When we built our house with its back entrance on Sheriff's Lane long ago, we cut off Miss Leila Pease's view of the town clock, a view she had long cherished and that had been of some usefulness. I am still sorry she lost it because of us. When Grace Ward mentioned politely and pointedly that we had Christmas lights in our windows toward Pierce Lane but none in windows toward Sheriff's

Lane, I went out and bought more lights, and then Grace could see not only the ordinary glow through our trees but also the special lights of Christmas.

The New Year came, then the long haul of winter cold, and a slow reluctant spring. In its own fashion, at last, July edged in, thick, soft, and dripping with fog. Arriving vacationers poured from the crowded ferries, cars proceeded almost bumper to bumper through the main streets of the larger towns. The big diesel sightseeing buses were back, turning with difficulty in narrow ways, blending their fumes with the exhausts of ordinary automobiles. Motorcycles were back, too, blasting and roaring. All the fumes were absorbed in the universality of fog, but fog now with less of saltiness than a reminder of city blocks. The encompassing reality, of course, was summer, impatient, teeming, straining, fretfully active summer.

Through the fog banks old houses, copses, open hills, boulders, and outlying shorelines loomed like ghosts, larger than reality, the fantasies of remembered summers past and gone.

The new summer was unlike the old, when Mrs. Dinsmore in a pale blue dress, white gloves, and with a parasol could come walking at her ease along North Water Street.

~

How describe the innocence and open simplicity of life on Martha's Vineyard as it used to be, so often surprising the summer people when they arrived for the first time?

People were secure in their sense of place and of what they had to do on some day of the week or season of the year. Their pace and activity were in the natural order of the Island, and they were set apart by their heritage from the oceanic world and their present occupations afloat and alongshore. They were insular but not provincial, and the first importance of the sense of home was that it flourished so naturally after generations of voyaging.

The relationship with the past survives a little still, in compromises the Island makes today. In 1793 young Thomas Dunham from Holmes Hole, the modern Vineyard Haven, chanced to be in Le Havre when Charlotte Corday was sent to the guillotine. First a heroine of the Revolution, then of the counter-Revolution, she was the one who stabbed the terrorist leader Marat to death in his bath. Perhaps Tom Dunham saw her and thought her beautiful, perhaps it was her story that touched his sense of romance when he was twenty-two; at any rate, she captured his imagination, and years afterward when at fifty-eight he had become a man of substance at home on Martha's Vineyard, he named an Indian-summer daughter of his own Charlotte Corday.

Charlotte's surname, Dunham, was not much used. When she taught at the Old Wood School in North Tisbury, her pupils knew her as Charlotte Corday. Not many of us nowadays can point out the site of the Old Wood School in its shady quietude at the fork of two little-used mossy roads, where the slight rustling of oak leaves in summer and the stir of wind in winter seem to make the silence more complete. The school was geographically central because this was politically correct, but it was not near any settled place, and therefore an unrealistic presence in those lonely oak woods even when the first class gathered in its single room.

As a boy I knew a retired whaleman, a lean, weathered figure with crinkly skin over the bones of his face and a slender gold ring in either ear, who had gone to school to Charlotte Corday, as he remembered her. This old whaleman called me "Bub," which was the fashion aboard whaleships in his time. He left the Old Wood School to ship aboard the *Morning Light* for a Pacific voyage, and at Talcahuano in Chile found the ship *Niger* and went aboard her to visit Charlotte Corday, who meanwhile had married Captain Nathan Jernegan and sailed with him. The way of the world was pretty much the way of the Island in those days, at least as to the oceanic oneness in which all was bound. Charlotte Corday was pregnant aboard the *Niger* and came ashore at Talcahuano to wait out her term. When the baby was born, a boy, the *Niger* came back for her. She said her baby would be a great comfort to her the rest of the voyage.

Vineyarders were less concerned with London, Paris, Berlin, and Rome than with Talcahuano, Paita, Hakodate, Ponape, Celebes, and so on, and these last were easier to get to, because they were where whaleships went. Yet home was always home, and it was put aboard a ship and taken wherever the ship might go.

Witnesses may be called to say how things used to be, from the remotest time. A young geologist the other day found in a lump of Gay Head clay a three-dimensional fossil flower dating from the Cretaceous period, or perhaps 130 million years ago. This is the oldest flower known to science, and it may be taken as a beginning mark of our history. Gay Head, westernmost promontory, is a storehouse of the past.

Another geologist, Barbara Blau Chamberlain, has discovered that in places on our Island the glacial debris is so thin that a qualified researcher can find a visible record of

95 million years, a self-history unique in New England. There is no doubting the interest or the seniority of our landscape, which deserves more respect than speculative land developers usually have for it.

For the earliest authentic written history one may look to the narrative of John Brereton, gentleman voyager, member of Bartholomew Gosnold's company in a "smalle barke of Dartmouth called the 'Concord,' " which entered Vineyard Sound in May 1602: "We stood a while like men ravished at the beauty and delicacie of this sweet soil . . . lakes of fresh water, of which we saw no end . . . meadoes very large and full of green grass . . . high timbered oaks . . . and such an incredible store of vines that we could not go for treading on them."

These vines were of wild grapes, and they led Captain Gosnold to christen the Island Martha's Vineyard for his daughter; or perhaps for his mother-in-law, Martha Golding, an influential lady who may have abetted his voyage. In 1642 came Thomas Mayhew, Jr., with an advance party of settlers. He, a historian's account goes,

being then a young scholar about 21 years of Age . . . became pastor of a new church society, but his English flock being but small, the Sphere was not large enough for so bright a star to move in. With great compassion he beheld the wretched Natives who were then several thousands on these Islands, perishing in utter Ignorance of the true God and eternal life, labouring under strange Delusions, Inchantments, and panick Fears of Devils whom they passionately worshipped . . .

But the Indian was not eager to be served, with one noteworthy exception. Living near the English settlement was a native called Hiacoomes. His descent was mean, his speech slow, and his countenance not very promising. He was looked on by the Indian sachems and others of their principal men as an object scarce worthy of their notice or regard.

It was the lowly, unpromising Hiacoomes, not courted by his own people, who found advantage in the friendship of the Englishmen. He became the instrument by which the Indians were persuaded to Christianity.

Many years later Hiacoomes was raised to Biblical rank in a poem by John Greenleaf Whittier. The "Sanchekontacket" of which the poem speaks was a Vineyard place name still current in the form "Sengekontacket." There was a farm of that name until a newcomer of sophisticated times, afraid that it might be too formidable for his milk customers, changed it to "Dairyland," a term well worn in modern American usage.

Whittier wrote:

> Sanchekontacket's isle of sand
> Was once my father's hunting land,
> Where zealous Hiacoomes stood, —
> The wild apostle of the wood,
> Shook from his soul the fear of harm,
> And trampled on the pow-wow's charm;
> Until the wizard's curses hung
> Suspended on his palsying tongue,
> And the fierce warrior grim and tall
> Trembled before the Forest Paul!

Now comes Manasseh Cutler, pausing a few years at Edgartown before pressing westward to help settle Ohio. From his journal, 1769: "My sloop Favorite from the mole of St. Nicholas laden with sugar which I had supposed lost, but she came into Vineyard Sound well-conditioned . . . Sat up singing. Began to sing by rule, the first time

. . . Whalemen fitted out for the season. Later I fitted half with Captain Pease."

This was the era of Atlantic whaling when an outfit need be only for a season and not for, say, four years, as when the ships went into the Pacific. Hector St. John Crèvecoeur, circa 1779, in his *Letters of an American Farmer*, writing of Martha's Vineyard:

> The moral conduct, prejudices and customs of a people who live two-thirds of the time at sea must naturally be different from that of their neighbors who live by cultivating the earth. That long abstemiousness to which the former are exposed, the breathing of saline air, the frequent repetitions of dangers, the boldness of the winds to which they are exposed; all these, one would imagine, must lead them while on shore to no small desire of inebriation, and a more eager pursuit of those pleasures of which they have been so long deprived and which they must soon forego . . . .
>
> On the contrary, all was peace here, and a general decency prevailed throughout; the reason I believe is that almost everyone is married, for they get wives very young, and the pleasure of returning to their families absorbs every other desire. The motives that lead them to the sea are very different from those of most other seafaring men; it is neither idleness nor profligacy that sends them to that element; it is a settled plan of life, a well-founded hope of earning a livelihood; it is that their soil is bad that they are early initiated to this profession, and if they were to stay at home, what would they do? . . . They have all, from the highest to the lowest, a singular keenness of judgment, unassisted by academical studies . . .

Nathaniel Hawthorne, in one of his *Twice-Told Tales*, "Chippings With a Chisel," tells of a discourse with one Wigglesworth, an itinerant stonecutter, at Edgartown in 1835, old age being so much the custom and deaths so widely spaced, that no resident plied this uncertain trade. "Discussion fell on the epitaph chosen by an infidel, so considered, who wished an avowal of his belief that the spirit would be extinguished like a flame, and that the nothingness whence he sprang would receive him again. Mr. Wigglesworth consulted me as to the propriety of enabling a dead man's dust to utter this dreadful creed . . ."

But in the Edgartown cemetery today the epitaph seems less than dreadful, fitting the creed of the naturalists in philosophy who do not regard themselves as infidels:

> By the force of vegitation
> I was raised to life and action
> When life and action that shall cease
> I shall return to the same source

Hawthorne continued his essay: "There was an old man by the name of Norton, noted throughout the Island for his great wealth, which he had accumulated by the exercise of strong and shrewd faculties, combined with a most penurious disposition. This wretched miser, conscious that he had not a friend to be mindful of him in his grave, had taken the needful precaution for posthumous remembrance by bespeaking an immense slab of white marble with a long epitaph in raised letters . . ."

This stone, also, is easily found today. The "old miser," Ichabod Norton, offered to distribute his property to his heirs before his death, but at a discount of twelve and a half percent. The heirs accepted the offer, satisfying Ichabod that he had made a profit of twelve and a half percent on his own estate. He won also the fame of an epitaph suggested by one of his heirs. Though it was cut on no stone, it lives on in Vineyard annals:

Here lies old twelve and a half percent.
The more he saved, the less he spent.
The less he spent, the more he craved,
Oh Lord, can Ichabod be saved?

In January 1844 my maternal grandfather, Henry W.
Beetle, then first mate on the ship *John Adams*, Bradford,
master, at Capetown from the Indian Ocean, addressed his
"Affectionate Wife": "Every day I feel more anxious to be
with you and in hopes to be by April . . . It is past 9
o'clock in the evening with us, and I am writing to you,
and the second mate to his father. We came in last evening,
today employed cleaning ship . . . I have not been on
shore yet and whether I go is uncertain. If I was sure I
would not get the scurvy I am sure I would not. What more
to write I do not know, for news I have none. I hear the
wind a-whistling on deck, and the Capt. ashore, which
gives me double duty tonight, but if I could while away
some of your time from pain or sorrow I would write until midnight."

Even after weeks at sea he would not go ashore and feel
land under his feet but for the fact that a stay on shore was
believed to prevent scurvy, the cause of which was then
unknown.

Herman Melville introduces a shipmate of the *Pequod*,
Ahab, master:

Next was Tashtego, an unmixed Indian from Gay Head,
the most westerly promontory of Martha's Vineyard,
where still exists the last remnant of a village of red men,
which has long supplied the neighboring Island of Nantucket with many of her most daring harpooners. In the
fishery they generally go by the genetic name of Gay
Headers. Tashtego's long, lean sable hair, his high cheek
bones and black rounding eyes — for an Indian, Oriental
in their largeness, but Antarctic in their glittering expres-

sion — all this proclaimed him an inheritor of the unviti-
ated blood of those proud warrior hunters . . . Tashtego
now hunted in the wake of the great whales of the sea, the
unerring harpoon of the son replacing the infallible arrow
of the sires. To look at the tawny brawn of his lithe snaky
limbs, you would almost have credited the superstitions
of some of the early Puritans and believed this wild Indian
to be a son of the Prince of the Powers of the Air.

Now one of many similar epitaphs in the West Side
cemetery at Edgartown, the sadness of an heroic epic
graven on marble:

HENRY
Son of
JOHN AND HARRIET FELLOWS
died on board ship
America
on the coast of New Holland
Nov. 26, 1841
AE 18 Yrs 3 Mos

He died upon the rolling wave
Far from his native shore
No parents stood beside his grave
Though we his loss deplore

From the *Vineyard Gazette*, May 11, 1859: "The good
ship Walter Scott, Henry Pease 2nd, master, left this port
for San Francisco, California, at 11½ o'clock on Monday
last. She takes with her thirty-six of our townsmen, besides
eight others belonging to the Island, and these men con-
stituted a great portion of the bone and muscle of the community. They have left many sad hearts behind them —
the hour of parting was a bitter hour — may that of reun-
ion be as blissful as that of their departure was grievous."

Epitaph on a very small stone in the West Side cemetery
at Edgartown, under a carving of a bird carrying a twig:

GRACE ANN COON
Born at the Sandwich Islands, August 9, 1853
Died May 1, 1855, at sea in Lat 40 degrees S
Long 78 Degrees West

Nathaniel Southgate Shaler, tall Kentuckian, Harvard University geologist, humanist, philosopher and scholar, writes in the *Atlantic Monthly*, 1874:

> Almost every face we meet on the broad shoulders of the seafaring people shows marks of character the sea alone can give. Most of them have something of the leonine look which comes from long habit of command; many are bronzed, with the deep, ingrained hue got only within the tropics which never fades again, . . . but seems as fixed as tattoo marks . . . A man gets a liberal education of a rude sort before he becomes a successful shipmaster. The sea is a searching examiner, ruthlessly plucking all who do not deserve success. Not the least of its lessons is content with small things and a reasonable interest and satisfaction in the moment . . .
>
> In a commercial sense . . . [Edgartown] is far advanced in decay; of all its whaleships which got from the sea the hard-earned fortunes of its people, there is but one left . . . But the thrift and cleanliness of the sailor is marked in every paving stone and shingle of the village. As soon as a mariner comes to fortune his first effort is to get a comfortable home, a big, square, roomy house which shall always be shipshape and well painted. I never thought so well of white paint before I saw these handsome houses, actually resplendent with a hue that is often merely garish in its uses . . . These comfortable houses, like those of New Bedford, mark a period of prosperity which has passed, never to return.
>
> In the new life which our growing fashion of summering by the sea is bringing to Martha's Vineyard, it is to be hoped that the pleasant traces of the old may be well

preserved. But lest it all be swept away, we advise our tourists who would see the best of their own land to see it for themselves.

⌒

In our first year at Edgartown, 1920, Betty and I often walked down in the evening to the ruined wharf at the foot of Main Street to look out at the harbor, listen to its restlessness, and to watch the afterglow deepening in the sky over Chappaquiddick. The wharf planks were broken and askew in places, still firm enough in others, a sea-stricken kind of ruin one liked because of the strength with which it had resisted time and the weather, and because of the historic quality it represented. We would sit on the caplog at the wharf's end nearest to the channel, watching the changing colors and the force of the current.

There was danger in the wreck of the timbers, and it must have been part of one's feeling, since this too was attributed to the sea. A year or so later, the postmaster fell through one of the gaps at night and was drowned.

I wonder why we did not see any finality in the ruin of the wharf, as Shaler had done. There was no promise at the time of any arresting of the process of decay, but we were not surprised when the future began shaping itself upon the background of the past, and the historic wharf of China trade under the Coffins and of whaling under the Osborns was rebuilt solidly for the purposes of a yacht club.

"The growing fashion of summering by the sea" had gained enormously since Shaler's day in what seemed a desirable evolution, advantageous all around, though in patterns of the new century. An observation of Nathaniel Hawthorne's might have been used, if one had thought of it, to symbolize a new departure: "For a few summer weeks it is good to live as if this world were heaven."

I don't recall that sermons were preached on the subject, but when advertising slogans came along, as they did in great numbers, they derived from a different school of expression. Someone had the notion of making the Island attractive by calling it the "Isle of Dreams," and thereafter threadbare sentimentality and fancy verbiage ran unchecked. Radio and television, of course, would attract such rot, as molasses used to attract flies.

To Betty and me there seemed to be security and protection in the fact of insularity. It did no harm that Martha's Vineyard was considered remote and difficult of access. Vessels of earlier centuries had gone into far seas without too much difficulty, though a good deal of time was required. A ship sailed, went where it was supposed to go, and came back again. But when Howard W. Spurr, then a wholesale grocery salesman, came from Boston shortly after the Civil War, he boarded "the cars" — at South Station, debarked at the railhead at Monument, later known as Monument Beach, near where the Cape Cod Canal now cuts through; took the stagecoach to Woods Hole, a packet from Woods Hole to Holmes Hole on the Vineyard; and a coach from there to Edgartown, where he met his future wife at a dance in the town hall. There were advantages in going and coming to and from Honolulu as against travel to and from Boston. Even religion experienced inconvenience on account of our geography, for early preachers coming by sailing packet were apt to be driven off course; they suffered from seasickness, and some were deceitfully put ashore on Chappaquiddick.

Knowing the past as we did, Betty and I had no anxiety about the future. We knew of the year 2000 as a symbolic date, but not in its present doomsday sense. It did not represent humanity's note of indebtedness coming due, or the fulfillment of any Faustian bargain. There would be fifty years more of boom and bust, inflation, war, population growth, and so on, before Barbara Ward and René Dubos were to write their book, *Only One Earth*, embodying the significance of the Stockholm Conference and warning solemnly, "If all man can offer to the decades ahead is the same combination of scientific drive, economic cupidity, and national arrogance, then we cannot rate very highly the chance of reaching the year 2000 with our planet still functioning safely and our humanity preserved."

It was quite a while, too, before I could take from my box at the post office yet another circular from the group known as Negative Population Growth, Inc., headed in black type: "TIME BOMB, POPULATION GROWTH PERILS," and continuing: "The final Armageddon will likely come . . . not from a nuclear holocaust but from a simple crush of people." The same point was made by John Hersey in his novel, *My Petition for More Space*.

The year 2000 — no later — was clearly the time of the predicted catastrophe. Armageddon had been overprophesied, but now we had a firm date. As we examined the situation at Edgartown we could see an accumulation of evidence.

In 1800 the town had 1226 inhabitants, a number that was to vary only slightly up or down until it stood at 1209 when the twentieth century came in. The population was 1190 when Betty and I arrived in 1920, and this number seemed about right, though no one would have objected to a few more, especially in winter when the streets were almost empty and business was slack.

By 1975 we had grown, most rapidly in recent decades,

to a new, all-time peak of 2128. This might not in itself impress an outsider, but when the total was added to the number of people in China and India for statistical purposes, one arrived at an astounding figure. There are places nearer than China or India that could be used to strengthen the point, but arguments are best clinched on a grand scale. We were not alone. We were caught in forces around the world that threatened to engulf us all. By the year 2000.

Population was not the only thing. Suddenly we found ourselves in Edgartown with a drugstore, our only real one, lacking the prized folk institution of a soda fountain. What had the god of economics wrought? The nature of our culture could be seen yielding to the advance hosts of Armageddon. Amenities running back beyond our time to Enoch Cornell's ice-cream saloon in Gothic Hall had been declared obsolete.

We remembered Bill Mendence and how he used to stand in the doorway of his Main Street tobacco shop and the ice-cream shop and soda fountain twinned to it. Bill, small and baldish, grinned like an innkeeper, observant of all who walked by — townspeople or summer visitors were not only customers but constituents.

All ages sat on wire stools at his soda fountain, sorted out as to time of day: school children in the afternoon; housewives and club women somewhat later, after they had been to the shops or at meetings listening to papers on Peru or Self-Help with Household Plumbing; loners and fishermen in the evening. Bill's place became a resort for deepwater fishermen from Noank and Stonington, among whom was their chronicler, Ellery Thompson, subject of a "Profile" in *The New Yorker* and then author of a book called *Draggerman's Haul*.

"At 8 P.M.," Ellery wrote in his book, "with the boats securely tied, while a gale of wind swept across the marshes outside the village, we were all gathered in Edna's ice-cream soda parlor, buying round after round of Edna's ice-cream sodas, knowing perfectly well we'd have bellyaches later."

Edna was Bill's daughter, a pioneer in the field of wider employment for women. The chocolate-covered ice-cream confection known as Eskimo Pie was introduced in Edgartown by Bill Mendence. In his place of business was a "public" telephone, not a booth or a coin-operated affair, but an old-fashioned telephone on the wall. Most people didn't have telephones then, and anyone could call up Mendence's, and either he or Edna would appoint one of the familiars of the establishment to go out, find the desired party, and bring him to the telephone, or perhaps give a message or an instruction of some kind. A minimal sum paid for this service.

Many coin-operated telephones have appeared in Edgartown through the years. For a while they were installed in blue-trimmed aluminum and glass booths, usually in pairs. Such a booth, lighted at night, was lashed by winds, sleet, and snow all winter long in the loneliness of the Harbor View veranda with not even a rocking chair to give it companionship, until some authority curtailed this proffer of communication. Climate had won out.

Our coin telephones are now on shelves attached to the outside of buildings in full view of the populace, so that anyone making or receiving a call becomes a public citizen, like Ralph Nader. But something about a telephone conversation induces a false sense of privacy that does not exist, and under this shield of imagined isolation the person holding the telephone assumes all kinds of intimate attitudes and expressions. He, mostly, but sometimes she, will seem to dispose of his or her feet in knots, study the sky with curious absorption, scratch his or her anatomy in places not usually scratched in public view, and dispense with conventions generally.

Advances in telephony are not always accepted by older inhabitants as real improvements. In the old days when Otis Burt moved from Middletown to the North Shore for a summer's fishing, he disconnected his telephone, wrapped it in a horse blanket and took it with him, reconnecting it in his summer quarters. When my brother and I were boys in our house, Fish Hook, in North Tisbury, which my father rightly said was the end of the line, our telephone was on a seventeen-party line, and our distinguishing "ring" was 35-33, which meant three long, very long, jingles of the telephone bell followed by three short ones. No one on the line could remain in ignorance of when we were being called, and it was always possible to get to the telephone from any part of our house before the bell stopped ringing. If anything, we had to wait for the bell to finish off.

If a pole was down somewhere between North Tisbury and the central office at Vineyard Haven, our line operated independently and, as I remember, proudly. We made more calls than usual, out of a spirit of emancipation. All we needed to do was to turn the little crank on the telephone box and we could open a domain of communication all the way from Orrin Look's farm way down on the state road, through Lambert's Cove to the Vineyard Sound shore, and up through Middletown to S. M. Mayhew's general store. Old-time telephone men say nothing has ever improved on what they refer to as the good old common battery system, which younger men say was the magneto system. It would even operate underwater.

When the company began eliminating the hand cranks and substituting instruments without them, a strong contingent of rural subscribers in West Tisbury petitioned against the change. When dials began to appear, most of us remained cool to them. Our exchange was last to be changed over, and we wouldn't have minded waiting even longer.

Dials did away with the operators who were uniquely helpful in town life. Our own Laura Paul, for instance, knew where everyone was, who everyone was, and what the special relationships of town and Island required. When dials came, the whole social order changed, and a communications center had to be set up at the airport in the geographical heart of the Island.

Many of us still miss Laura and her helpfulness. A friend told me the other day that he experienced such difficulty with a long-distance call that he got himself connected to his brother-in-law in Nicaragua, who by means of international prestige then put through to the desired party. In the old days we couldn't call on Nicaragua or any other outlying place but had to go it alone.

My automobile, a vexed Nova that I have a good deal to say about from time to time, lost its transmission again the other day, and there I was, a mile or so out of Vineyard Haven on the county road. I walked to a nearby house and asked to use the telephone, a request quickly granted, but a telephone directory could not be found. I dialed the information operator and asked for the number by which I could get the biggest garage in Vineyard Haven. The operator told me crisply that she didn't know. An odd lapse, I thought. Then she said, "I'm in Boston." Of course she was. No longer just down the street.

We used to have our own resident telephone managers,

always available to serve on committees and assist the Red Cross or the Chamber of Commerce. They brought new releases to the *Gazette* office and were an image of the Bell System. Now the "local" manager is across Vineyard Sound in Falmouth, and we have no way of knowing whether he wears a daily carnation in his buttonhole.

Across from Bill Mendence's stood the newspaper, cigar, and candy store of Leroy Tilton and his wife, Jessie. Their back-room parlor with neat little tables and chairs won a loyal patronage, and they claimed their ice cream was better than Bill's because they made it themselves. Later, for reasons of economy, they had theirs shipped in from New Bedford also, and still said it was better.

Jessie Tilton in her youth had played Little Meenie on tour with Joseph Jefferson's *Rip Van Winkle* company. Newcomers in the summer colony, knowing for sure only that she had been on the stage, reported that she had been one of the original Flora Dora girls, the plausibility of the story giving it a long life. Mrs. Tilton affected indifference to the stuffy people in town, but she remarked more than once, "It's all right for them to wheel their bastards down Main Street but not for me to have toured with Joe Jefferson."

Her husband, tall, dark, taciturn by habit, shared some of her temperament. They both liked to insult people they thought should be insulted. All copies of the *New York Times* on their counter were reserved for regular customers, and one time when Charles Merz, a *Times* editor, visiting in town, picked one up, Leroy exclaimed loudly, "Put that down!"

"Does anyone else in town sell the *Times*?" Mr. Merz asked.

"No one else is foolish enough," replied Mr. Tilton.

We were all characters in those days. It was easy to slip into being one, and nicknames helped: Joe Twotail, who had reported seeing a rat with two tails; Popcorn Harry, Joe Monk, Captain Spike, Joe Nose, Dr. Bug, Hoppy King. A new school teacher in all innocence once referred to Hoppy King as "Mr. Hopkins King."

It was easy to get into the grocery business; what you needed most was sawdust on the floor, a long white market-man's coat, and straw sleeveguards. It helped, but was not necessary, for you to settle your accounts as often as twice a year.

John Bent, who was born in Lisbon, kept a grocery store on Lower Main Street. His father had been a decorator of churches, and John exercised an artistic talent by painting signs for his store. One of them was a black-mustached portrait he had painted of himself wheeling a barrow full of vegetables, with the legend "Fresh from Bent's Farm Daily." They were fresh all right, but the farm was really a market garden.

Once when I happened into John's store he was sculpting the statue of a nymph blowing a blast on a seashell. He had dug a trench in the back yard, filled it with a home mix of cement in which ashes were a frugal ingredient, and when the block was hardened had taken to it his mallet and chisel. Years later Marshall Shepard and I wooed the completed statue from John's estate for the Dukes County Historical Society, but some curator or other threw it out.

One of John's notices in the *Gazette*:

To my dear friends:
I wish you would be kind enough not to throw any de-cayed apples at my cat. He does not do any harm to you in

the middle of the road. If you have anything against me I had rather you throw apples at me rather than at my poor cat. He can't help what I do.

> Yours truly,
> John Bent

John yielded slowly to the overwhelming odds of his own lengthening age and of competition by both the new chain store and California's Imperial Valley and its colorful produce.

Another grocery was kept in an old mansion on Summer Street by Manuel Silva, Jr., a hard-muscled and spunky five-foot veteran of whaling. His profanity was wonderful, and summer customers from Scarsdale and such places liked it, because if the man who weighed out your sugar had been chased by warriors in the South Pacific and survived several hurricanes, you appreciated a warrant of his authenticity.

The paper store and post office were in the same block, and since everyone went to both places at least once a day you could stand around and keep track of town affairs. Our favorite clerk at the post office was Lady Katherine Graham, a slender, pretty woman of unfailing courtesy. She had never claimed the title because Scotland was so far away and her father had died long ago.

Bill Cottle's candy and tobacco store, poolroom in the rear, stood a block up from Tilton's across the street. Bill had sailed two Pacific whaling voyages as a young man, and later he had fired the locomotive *Active* on the narrow-gauge railroad that ran along the beach between Edgartown and Oak Bluffs. Betty and I liked to buy a bag of Bill's chocolate creams to take with us to the new movie theater one door down the street, the one that later burned down, but not before the Golden Age had fallen away.

It was in Bill's place that Eddie Pease, on the eve of his marriage to a wealthy and considerably older widow, remarked to those present as he gave out cigars, "Nobody can say that it's *purely* a love match." His bride to be, known familiarly as Aunt Flo, had made her own comment on the approaching nuptials when she recalled how Eddie Pease's mother had wheeled him past her parlor windows in a baby carriage, so many years earlier, when she and her husband were looking out: "I wonder what Elroy would have said if I had told him that some day I was going to marry that baby."

As far back as I can remember, there were two barber shops in town, and one of them had two barbers kept busy all summer long. The shop just off Main Street on North Water belonged to Clarence A. Dexter — initials C.A.D. — and of course was known as Cad's, just as he was known as Cad and not by any other name. It was smaller than you would think, but it accommodated a row of chairs along one wall where the hatrack stood, and a table with old and new papers and magazines. The other large wall was given over mostly to an enormous still-life painting, the work of Cad himself, which included about all generally recognized fruits from watermelons to grapes. Cad thought highly of this work and I suppose rightly so, especially if judged by area. A back room, adequate for cribbage games, was usually devoted to that use. The smells, back and front, were of tobacco smoke, steamy rubber boots, bay rum, witch hazel, Lucky Tiger, Zepp's Dandruff Cure and, all winter long, a hot sheet iron stove.

Diagonally across the street at our famous Four Corners — as if there were not almost always four corners at a conventional intersection — Ed Nichols, the Sanitary Barber, as he advertised himself in the *Gazette*, catered to customers who preferred him or would have had to wait for a turn at Cad's. Ed belonged to an older generation, the sociability of his shop accordingly diluted. When Ed died, Dr. Walker's drugstore moved into the premises and became the first modern store of its kind in town.

By this time Bill Mendence had been shoaled off by progress, mainly because of age and the innovation of making Main Street a one-way passage going down, which left him on what turned out to be the wrong side. Bill was entirely willing to reshape his life. He lived at Mrs. Mellen's, where the school teachers boarded, and walked downtown to enjoy the afternoon slope of his years and the congenial occupation of reminiscence. He enjoyed being a patriarch and beginning his sentences, "Do you remember when . . . ?"

The arrival of the drugstore at the Four Corners coincided with the new era of enterprise and enlightenment following World War I. The town was ready for the fresh spirit that the store and its furnishings so boldly represented. Glasses, straws, faucets, ice cream, napkins — everything had been provided for in or on the imitation marble soda bar (or it might have been real marble way back then) so that the operator did not have to turn around. I don't know whether in earlier years he had "jerked" a soda, but now he did. Corson's drugstore in New Bedford, the first one I knew, had faucets behind the clerk, all bearing the name of a flavor except one, which was marked "Don't Care." If you asked for that, you got pineapple.

Conversations at the new Four Corner drugstore, which eventually became Pete's, promoted an easy, continuing exchange of town news, much of which was accurate, and embraced all subjects from politics to religion, steamboat service, weather, of course, and the problems not only of democracy but of philosophy.

Long afterward, when Pete Vincent had sold the store, he would say that in strict accounting terms the fountain had never paid for its keep and its service. The profit it yielded had to be counted in a different coin, and the totals, year by year, were considerable and of great account to the community.

The values that became important in the decades following World War II were increasingly severe and practical. Each square foot of floor space in a drugstore was required to yield the maximum return. Sociability, politics, and the historic "time of day" gossip yielded to cash register figures. The computer was still in the future but not far. Through the years when Pete owned the store, and when Miss Susan Beetle was pharmacist, this was as near the heart of the town as you were likely to get.

Miss Beetle, straight of figure and always cordial, seemed a New England folk lore sort of person. She was the first licensed woman pharmacist in the state, and her score on the examination had been phenomenal. She and I were distant cousins, her Beetle branch having split off after the second Christopher, prior to 1800, but she had known my grandfather and referred to him as Uncle Henry. I mention this as an instance of the kinology — William Allen White's term — which has had its importance in all small towns and will soon be lost in the world of mass.

Betty and I would go downtown in the evening at any time before ten o'clock, and peer into an oak-framed showcase containing different varieties of chocolates. Miss Beetle would help us choose what we wanted, so many lime centers, so many nougats and caramels, easy on the raspberry centers, and so on. This was the final chapter of such individual choice, when you could make your own selection every time, before conformity closed out such options.

There was not much evening trade at the drugstore except in summer, even though downtown was livelier than now, with the sidewheeler *Uncatena* arriving from New Bedford after dark, and the post office keeping open until eight o'clock so that we could get our late mail, if any. Though customers might be scarce, the drugstore, always lighted and nicely warm, attracted a gathering of what might be called strays: politicians in season, children on errands, traveling salesmen (then known as drummers), husbands whose wives were entertaining a sewing circle or a church society. An occasional semivagrant might show up, too. This was the real night life that has gone in the era of urban nocturnal entertainment.

Once it was believed that a soda jerker must be male and of an informed, worldly wisdom. He enjoyed and practiced political awareness — though was often found to be mistaken when the votes were counted — gave medical advice of an informal kind, dispensed Bromo-Seltzer with style, and helped circulate the latest topical jokes. Not until World War II was it discovered that he could be displaced by a pretty girl, young but not too young, who was even better with a blister or taking a foreign object out of a stranger's eye. This was also the period when girls appeared as clerks in chain stores, and even as meat cutters, before they reached their ultimate destiny at the checkout counter.

The soda fountain did not disappear because of a lack of demand or a lack of custom but was a victim of modern accounting methods. I think the business schools did it in. Even as the ice-cream cone escalated in price it escalated in popularity. At fifty cents, then sixty, it would outsell yesterday's cones that, if your memory was good, you knew cost only a nickel. Exiled from the drugstore, the ice-cream cone turned up almost everywhere else, so that every shopkeeper had a sign on the door: "No Food, No Dogs, No Bare Feet." Ice-cream cones dripped, and hamburgers or hot dogs left mustard stains.

Dogs found their old freedoms restricted. They were no longer allowed near the vegetable displays in front of grocery stores and could not have fights with other dogs on street corners. A new law provided for an animal-control officer who, though usually good-natured and a conversationalist, found it necessary to pick up a certain number of dogs. Summer people at times complained that friendly dogs were vicious, or complained about the barking, which had been one of the authentic small-town noises left after the disappearance of mooing cows.

So came the era of lost things, lost establishments, lost characters: no iceman any more, no milkman, no poolroom, no watering trough, of course — the last one had been planted with geraniums as long ago as the year Betty and I arrived.

Barber shops, one might say, were done in by an unfortunate lapse of fashion that no longer equated long hair and whiskers with disuse of shower or tub. Only a little while ago, as I think of years, I would wait outside Jordan's barber shop, formerly Cad Dexter's, at eight A.M. every Friday so that I might be the first customer and avoid what might be a long, though not unsociable, wait. Almost on the minute of eight George Jordan would come up, putt-putting on his motorbike, ready for a busy day. Sometimes there would be one or two, or even three, early customers ahead of me in the morning twilight, and I would resign and try again on Saturday at eight.

The dwindling of business occurred rapidly. Soon only one barber chair was operative. George went away, and his father would sit reading the *Boston Globe* and watching passers-by through the shop window, until at last he decided he would be better off at home.

This particular loss is being made good by young Rick Harrington, who has added a genuine barber shop to his hairdressing salon. A fine old-fashioned barber pole is his pride. I think this represents a professional spirit and recognition of the masculine tradition rather than an instance of business enterprise alone.

No one expected to be without a milkman. There were so many of them in the old days, each serving his own customers, who came down through the generations as if attached to a family tree. Arthur Norton was ours, and we always looked forward to his arrival at our gate in Sheriff's Lane, at first with his horse and wagon, later with his truck. The first change occurred during World War II when the government decided that, to save gasoline, milkmen must drive their routes only on alternate days. On the odd days most of us felt lost, especially if the household milk supply had run out. But we also wanted the morning greeting and early news.

A lot of townspeople began buying milk at the stores, bottles were replaced entirely by cartons, farmers gave up keeping cows because there were other ways of making a living with lighter work and easier hours. Competition, instead of being local with different milkmen and sets of customers, became national, with two-quart cartons arriving by truck at the chain stores, good for several days when kept in the kitchen refrigerator. Milk in cartons no longer gave notice of springtime by turning yellow at the top, showing that the cows had found new grass in the pastures and were grazing a longer and sunnier day. Most people no longer remembered, and even springtime lost an ancient household meaning that had brought poetry along with it.

The old-style movie theater has gone, too; church suppers are scarcer, and most holiday exercises draw smaller crowds. So much of town life that we possessed as genuinely our own, that pulled on us like the moon and tides, has been taken from us without recourse. A new generation grows up believing that it is living in better times. We begin to wonder if our passing will be noticed, or who will imaginably have time to notice.

It seems a strange fate, not to be missed, and strangest of all to think that we will have no successors. All the characters I remember and have mentioned, others too, had predecessors running far back in time, shaping the quality and continuity of town life, but their role has been written out of the script, and no one of their kind comes after them.

꙰

The DEQE held a prehearing conference in Boston on our Harbor View and Starbuck's Neck case. I didn't attend, not having a legal mind. Thirteen were present, and I name some of them out of respect for their impressiveness: Stanley H. Rudman, Esq., of Guterman, Horvitz, Rubin and Rudman, and Andrew J. Newman of the same firm but without the "Esq."; Jeremiah F. Healy III of Withington,

Cross, Park and Groden; Donald Connors of Tyler, Reynolds and Craig, and of course a supporting cast.

Jerry Healy represented us, Mr. Rudman and Mr. Newman the Harbor View, and Mr. Connors the Martha's Vineyard Commission. Thomas Powers, Esq., ran things for the DEQE. I suppose that having only three "Esq.'s" present may have operated on the side of economy.

It was Mr. Powers, I suppose, who ruled, on the authority of his department, that our side could not submit any evidence as to the regulations of the Martha's Vineyard Commission and therefore as to the fact that the wetland at Starbuck's Neck fell within the shore zone of the coastal district, although Jerry Healy made an offer of proof.

Both the commission and the DEQE were established by the same legislature, but on different days and apparently on different principles or different expediencies — or a blend of the two, which, knowing the Massachusetts state government, I think more likely. The blank wall between one law and another is a matter of comment only to non-lawyers. One way lawyers make money is by interpreting, though seldom wholly clarifying, the contradictions a layman often thinks must have been introduced into the statutes for that purpose.

John Sullivan, it turned out, was quite right in what he had told us at the site. The DEQE is not interested in ecology under the Wetlands Protection Act, though I suppose that under some other act it may be. This is frustrating to those who believe that ecology, like peace, cannot be divided.

Everyone who attended the prehearing conference went home again, and the lawyers marked down their time and expense. Jerry Healy thought that since the decision of the DEQE was so clearly predictable, we had best waive a formal hearing and take the matter directly to the courts on an agreed statement of facts. We were not aware at the time that not agreeing to any statement of facts is a tactical resource of what tradition still likes to call "a smart lawyer." This made no difference, though, because later we went ahead with a hearing anyway.

GRAHAM AND I walked out this morning with Edie Blake and her camera, along Pease's Point Way, in the aftermath of a sweet autumnal rain. We were going to explore and photograph Ox Pond Meadow, not a real meadow any longer, but old pastureland allowed to lie at ease with time and the will of the seasons. Much of the land had known the plough, some trailed off wetly into salt marsh, and some had been grazed over by sheep, cows, and the oxen of the place name.

Now sturdy wildflowers grow among a company of ruddy grasses that gleam when they are wet, small cedars, blackberry runners, thickets of bayberry, wild roses, even some strays from nearby gardens. A long, easy slope reaches to the marsh and a winding lagoon where great blue heron stalk or wade, samphire and sea lavender bloom, and autumn flames against blue sky and sea.

The meadow represents no design of nature, but what René Dubos has called symbiosis between earth and humankind, as in the English countryside where "the prodigious efforts of the settlers and farmers have created an astonishing diversity of eco-systems that appear natural only because they are familiar." In a few generations the land had become "a pleasing and highly diversified eco-system, its ditches and hedges harboring an immense variety of plants, insects, songbirds, rodents and larger mammals." It came to be regarded as a "natural" environment.

I could accept this, but not what came next. Modern practice, Dubos wrote, required that "ditches, hedges and trees must go in order to make possible the creation of larger tracts of land, more compatible with the use of high-powered agricultural equipment. The change is destroying habitats for the many kinds of wild animals and plants that lived in the hedged enclosures, but the open fields will certainly develop their own flora and fauna and, furthermore, have the advantage of permitting large sweeps of vision."

My sympathies are with the dispossessed, the fauna and flora so long and so beautifully accommodated, and I do not think that broad, open fields regularly subdued by high-powered agricultural equipment can produce habitats for wildlife of any account whatever. Of course I am on the defensive, ready to rise against all changes that impose conformity upon native land and that injure or deprive or kill the long-existing life of the land, whether one may narrowly define it as "natural" or as the working of a now outdated symbiosis. Our war at Starbuck's Neck involves this issue and I take it as a symbol that stands for all.

The rain had been heavy enough to leave puddles, and some of them Edie and I sloshed through, rather than walk unevenly on higher ground at the sides as Graham did. Edie inquired suddenly, "Aren't you scuffing your feet?" She is usefully frank at times.

"Actually I am not scuffing my feet," I said.

"Actually not? Then how?"

Well, it was my rubbers. They didn't exactly fit. They dragged at the heel. Rubbers come nowadays not in sizes but in size ranges, and you guess what will most nearly suit you. I had guessed wrong. In my youth things were different. You asked for and received rubbers that fitted your shoes, size for size.

I found myself diverging from the symbiosis between man and nature to that of man and scientific technology in the postindustrial age. René Dubos, I remembered, had come to the same crossroads.

He views the middle of the twentieth century as the watershed in the social adjustment between human beings and the environment. The 1933 World's Fair had brazenly proclaimed the gospel of increased wealth and living standards: "Science Discovers, Industry Applies, Man Conforms," but today, Dubos wrote, "No one would dare state . . . that humankind must conform to or fall in step with scientific or technological dictates."

I wondered if he had bought any rubbers lately.

It seemed to me that the age of scientific technology, after making a lot of promises, had begun taking a good many of them back. Rubbers were one small example. I don't know exactly when the hedging began, but I do know that day before yesterday in a cold wind, Graham and I sat on the front seat of my Chevrolet Nova, almost new, and began the enterprise of getting started and safely out of Sheriff's Lane.

There were years in my experience when you started your engine and, poof, you were off, but the instructions for starting my car leave out the "poof" and are complicated. You put your foot on the accelerator, turn the ignition key to crank the engines, and if the engine starts, you wait thirty seconds.

But what invariably happens, so far, I find to be different. The engine is reluctant about starting, then starts, falters, and comes to a dead stop. I must now repeat the procedure, and there are usually three or four repetitions. I am enough a victim of the modern temper to find thirty seconds an irksome time to wait, especially when I must begin reckoning over again after a series of false starts. Getting as far as twenty-nine seconds to no avail is like getting sent back in the ancient game of Parcheesi. "Take a little time — count five and twenty, Tattycoram," says Mr. Meagles in *Little Dorrit*. But surely we are more emancipated than that.

The procedure required to start my Nova is more convenient than the cranking of our first Buick in 1920, but our first Plymouth, circa 1935, would be off like a streak.

Of course I couldn't start my car at all without Graham's cooperation. Seat belts are not adapted to his use, and for that reason we keep two of the three in the front seat buckled all the time. Nevertheless, some built-in demon will cause internal buzzing and the red-light instruction, "Fasten Seat Belts," just as if they were not already fastened.

I glance at Graham on the front seat beside me and he

acknowledges my look with a slight change of expression. He shifts his weight slightly or perhaps draws a deep breath. The buzzing stops. The red light subsides. Graham, judging precisely the degree of effort required, has set us free to move.

Sheriff's Lane has an upward slope toward Pease's Point Way, which it enters over a kind of hump. We need power and momentum to negotiate the final ascent. We almost have it. The engine picks up. We are gaining. Maybe we'll make it. Then, toward the last twenty feet or so, we go faster and faster. We'll be popping out into Pease's Point Way like the food that's shot from guns unless I do something quickly. Of course I have my foot firmly on the brake, but the instruction book has warned me that "the idle speed" I had at the start and needed to get uphill "may be reduced by slightly depressing the accelerator pedal." How can I change from brake to accelerator in the brief moment before we emerge from behind H. L. Butler's tall privet hedge into that street of fast, impetuous travel, Pease's Point Way?

So far Graham and I have scored successes, some of them narrow. I had supposed that separate functions were assigned to brake and accelerator, and dependably so. The confusion troubles me. There is, however, more to my complaint against General Motors in this sophisticated period of the postindustrial age.

I was standing in the lane with Al West, head of the concern that sold me the car, and he remarked that three of the practically new tires were badly weather-checked. He didn't think I would have a blowout, but pretty soon I would very likely find myself with a flat tire.

"Tires," said Al, "are the only part of the car that we

don't guarantee. These are Uniroyal tires, and the distributor is over in Buzzard's Bay. I'll call him up."

Of course I knew about Buzzard's Bay: "town, Barnstable County, E. Massachusetts; on Cape Cod Canal near the entrance of inlet; pop.: 2170." It really isn't a town, because there isn't enough of it to be a town. The train used to stop there, when there was a train, and you changed cars for the Woods Hole branch.

To reach Buzzard's Bay I would need to drive six miles to the ferry terminal, pay $13.25 for a round-trip ticket if I went in the off-season and did not travel on Friday or Saturday, and drive, I would guess, twenty miles from Woods Hole to Buzzard's Bay, stop somewhere for lunch, and twenty miles back to Woods Hole. There used to be a woman in Buzzard's Bay who raised African violets, but I was not in the market for an African violet, and she might not be still living.

I telephoned the Uniroyal distributor and gave him the story of my tires and the weather-checking.

"There's no doubt you've got something coming to you," he said. "What we do, we measure the tread of the tire to see how much wear you've had out of it, and then we make allowance accordingly."

I weighed all the circumstances and decided that the journey to Buzzard's Bay would not be worth the allowance I would be likely to get. I looked back ruefully upon my years of automotive experience during which a guarantee of the tires came with the car, the manufacturer having contracted for the best buy he could get in tires. But some tire manufacturers complained that they were being left out, and the government sided with them, and said that automobile makers would have to spread their business around, as if all tires were of equal merit and all that mattered was price. I think General Motors knew what it was doing when it wouldn't guarantee my Uniroyals. There were three or four different makes that I would have preferred.

I will now turn to the matter of my General Electric refrigerator and General Electric furnace.

The first G.E. refrigerator in our house many years ago had a monitor top that made us think of the alembics and such effects of medieval sorcerers. After we had owned the refrigerator for a while it began to freeze its contents solid. We had bought the "big box," as he liked to call it, from a dealer on Martha's Vineyard, but the distributor was in Providence. I still have some letters we exchanged on the subject.

October 9, 1935, from the distributor: "On January 7th we rendered you an invoice for $25.75 for a new replacement unit for your refrigerator. We have made several special trips at considerable expense to give you attention and have issued you periodic statements for this balance."

October 11, 1935, from me to the distributor: "In the early summer, before we turned our house over to tenants for summer rental, this unit failed to stop freezing at the proper time and froze the contents of the refrigerator solid. A week ago when we returned to our house for the first time since spring, the unit did the same thing, spoiling a considerable amount of food."

November 29, 1935, from the distributor: "We are quite anxious to have that January 7, 1935, account for unit recently placed on your General Electric refrigerator paid before the middle of December. That isn't very far away but we do hope to hear from you before that time."

There is a gap here, and I don't recall what happened next. I think that eventually we got a unit that did not freeze the contents of the "big box." I marvel at how polite we all were, and how those sums loomed that now seem small. A learned young man used to come from the regional distributor's office in Providence on Saturdays, and we had scientific discussions in our kitchen. Whether he went on later into computers or nuclear power I can't say.

The most recent in our succession of G.E. refrigerators is a model having an interior arrangement on the principle of the lazy Susan. The shelves, each a half-circle, revolve, so that no matter where you put the mayonnaise or olives or cheese, a turn of the shelf will bring the desired item to the front. I soon found that so far as I was concerned it was as easy to reach in as it was to revolve the shelf. Whatever fun there might be in exercising the lazy Susan soon wore off, and I forgot it entirely.

Many years passed, eleven or twelve, so that it is necessary to fade out and fade in again to allow the passage of time its free term, like a chapter in Virginia Woolf. Now the door latches of both the refrigerator compartments went slack, allowing the doors to swing as they listeth.

The original dealer was no longer in business, and his successor showed a lack of interest in our problem. He couldn't do anything about the latches anyway because "they don't make 'em any more." They make different latches, not like these, with big heraldic bank vault handles and a G.E. escutcheon. Graham and I had an electric refrigerator that functioned about as well as ever but was useless because the doors swung open.

I tried a couple of devices to keep the main door closed, and found that a snow shovel worked best of all, leaned against the door with its blade edge gripping the kitchen floor. This, however, got in the way too much to serve as a permanent solution.

Finally I consulted our friend Stanley Strelecki, who made no big thing of a successful contrivance, though he had to wait for the arrival of parts. He drilled holes in the two doors and corresponding holes around the corner in the side of the refrigerator, then affixed hasps that, when a door was pushed forcefully shut, would engage a metal post on the side. This is a jury rig in the postindustrial age but it has an ingenuity that outwits the current fashion of obsolescence. I will say that only a solid kick with my foot will now close the lower refrigerator door, and the sound of the crash is not what one would like in a well-regulated home. Fortunately, Graham is not afraid of it, nor of thunder and lightning either, though a distant pop I would not otherwise notice is likely to send him scurrying.

When one of the posts installed by Stan broke off, perhaps from metal fatigue, I threw a line over an overhead heating pipe and hung a sashweight on the far end, fastening the near end to the door, which is thus kept tightly closed.

One other G.E. experience belongs here. Some years ago, having consulted our friend George-Henry Madeiros, who knew all about heating problems, we contracted to buy a General Electric hot water heating system. This proved to be the last hot water G.E. furnace on the Island of Martha's Vineyard and for all I know, in the country. General Electric had decided not to make any more, though hot water heat, I say, is more equable, better sustained, and more economical in the long run than forced-circulation hot air with its ups, downs, and drafts.

So, by the time the furnace began operating it was already an orphan. Though not quite, since George-Henry had been entrusted with the inner secrets of the G.E. hot water furnace and had not yet taken them to the grave. He made one gentle comment to me, "A man works all his life to handle a G.E. agency and gets word from the company that it is going out of wet heat."

George-Henry had looked around enough to know the times in which he and I were living. It was his view that the Depression years were the best time, the time we all like to look back upon with fondness. If you had a dollar it was really a dollar you had; and not a corporation in the country but would go out of its way to assist you, or sell you something. I can see him now, George-Henry with his quiet smile and wisdom, leaning back against the wall in a chair in Manuel Jordan's barber shop, discoursing about the Golden Age. A man could drive up to any filling station pump, yell "Ten!" and get ten cents worth of gasoline. And his windshield wiped for him, too.

In bitter winter weather nowadays I wake at night and wonder if the furnace is going to respond with its efficient click when the thermostat calls for heat. Who knows? George-Henry has gone, his philosophy and the G.E. secrets with him.

In big things and little things experience drives home the same lesson: They don't make 'em any more. They make something else, and something else is going to cost you money.

A little thing in this extremely large category: When Gillette began selling its band-type Techmatic razor, I bought one and liked it. Now and then I need a new cartridge, and the other day in Paul's drugstore I couldn't find one. The display rack offered, instead, cartridges for something more recent, an adjustable type of Techmatic.

I spoke to Paul about this. I said mine was a plain, uncomplicated razor and I wanted to keep it so.

"They're all coming through that way now," he said.

Economic law has always said that each satisfaction creates a demand for another and a higher one; but nowadays the compulsion and promise outrun the performance. You can't count on getting one rung higher. You'd as soon go down a little.

These are certain cardinal rules of the civilization of which I am, though unwillingly, a part:

> They don't make 'em any more.
> They're all coming through that way now.
> Fifteen cents off with coupon.
> A hundred percent pure (reconstituted).
> Fits all sizes.
> Batteries not included.
> No deposit, no return.
> Lowest in calories.
> Professionally dry clean only.
> Do not exceed recommended dosage.
> Dispose of carefully — don't litter!
> Finance charge of 1.5 percent, which is an annual rate of 18 percent.

I think of Samuel Keniston's farewell to the editorial duties of the *Vineyard Gazette* when he retired long, long ago. The profession, he wrote, was "not only not a bed of roses but in one way or another it is about as plentifully studded with thorns as the size of the bed will permit. Not great, jagged tenpenny spikes that let daylight through the victim and tear the flesh from his bones, but little pricks and splinters and pins that fret and harass and annoy but are neither big enough to hack away at nor important enough even to mention."

And here I am, mentioning just such annoyances in the broader context of the postindustrial age. I feel a kind of embarrassment as if, having magnified a nuisance by raising my voice a little, I may have sounded a call to the barricades and, looking around, found — as expected — that nobody was following or possibly would follow. "Neither big enough to hack away at nor important enough even to mention." But more of them every day.

Edith Blake and I had reached the gray, knotty rail fence that borders Ox Pond Meadow at the southern end. The air was a little warm and a little cool after the rain. We had parted company with René Dubos, even diverged widely, and it was good to be back with him again, contemplating this afternoon expanse of nature's one-time partnership with man, this happy accident, this anachronism in our lifetime, outlawed by modern technology's accomplishment and purpose, and by economics, or mostly so. We looked affectionately at the vista over Ox Pond Meadow, memorial to the lost symbiosis between us and the environment around us.

The lemon-tinted glow of sunlight yielded to the rising blush of clouds and sky above the sea, out toward a sharp horizon line. The tawny grasses sprawled, the tangle of wild roses, bayberry, and blackberry runners glistened, gulls soared above the marshes with the least movement of their wings. Graham had caught up with us and now bounded into the open territory of the meadow, pursuing a smell here or there, but nothing so definite as a rabbit.

The abundant life of Ox Pond Meadow is like that — small, elusive, secret — and we could imagine that along with all else there must remain some magic of the sturdy breed of humankind that achieved, without seeking or knowing, a symbiosis with the earth, gone forever, but in Ox Pond Meadow memorialized and each year a little bit more than remembered.

～

I stopped for the hitchhiker just beyond the turn into the Old Edgartown Road, as it used to be called to distinguish it from the newer Beach Road, which dates only from 1872. Now it is just the "back road" because time's distinctions get lost, to the regret of the small number who, like myself, knew them in childhood and hated to see them go.

The hitchhiker fitted no roadside type. He appeared respectable — no long hair or beard — and Dr. Gallup or any of the others would have been glad to learn his opinion on any subject. Added to his respectability he had the anonymity of the common man, a fact that ironically made him conspicuous in a gentle way. Almost always, what you have that is of different value is the very quality that tends to depreciate the value.

He started to open the front door of my car, and I stopped him before he could discover for himself that the door would not open. I had sideswiped a telephone pole in the dark of night while under the impression that I was being careful.

"You'll have to get in back," I said.

He opened a rear door, but he didn't get in.

He said, "I can't ride with you. I've got on my good pants." As he stepped on the curb again he added, "Have a good day."

I didn't think his pants looked *that* good, but the judgment was for him to make, not for me. I am less strict
about such matters, not only because one's standards tend
to sag with the passing of time and comforts of country
living, but also because I am addicted to dogs. Dogs tend
to justify a particular kind of housekeeping.

Two had been occupying my back seat recently —
Graham, of course, and his friend Ellie, a spayed English
setter, white with orange spots. Ellie likes cars so much
that I allow her to lie in mine when it is parked at the back
gate in Sheriff's Lane. A neighbor remarked that this must
be the most expensive kennel in regular usage. I thought,
yes, but it gets less expensive daily, what with the rapid
inroads of depreciation.

Soaking rains had fallen during the week, so that the
dogs, getting in and out of the car easily but not grace-
fully, and usually in a hurry, had spread a good deal of
brown sediment, or alluvium. They had also jumped back
and forth between front and back seats as occasion demanded, and had taken the quickest method of reaching
whatever window they were constrained to look out of.
The net effect upon the seats was that of a mosaic, whorled,
ridged, and layered, ready to be transferred in a simpler
manner than that of decalcomania to the navy blue pants
of a hitchhiker. Why, then, was I offended because the
hitchhiker had rebuffed me? If he had sat in my car, his
wife would certainly have demanded to know where he
had been.

I was not really offended, although in this modern
world, so well informed on the subject of rejections, any
rejection whatever is not to be taken without subsequent
analysis and often with self-reproach, which in my case I

might well have transferred to the hitchhiker and his family. Rejection is one of the great themes of the modern novel; it troubles educators and parents, and gives employment to social workers. And I could recall no other instance of rejection by a hitchhiker. My case was unique, and I knew I ought to be introspective about it.

Like automobile, like house, I thought guiltily. When guilt turns up you had better get at it quickly to prevent the warping of your personality.

It is not in my philosophy to live in a house in which a dog cannot lie on the couch in the living room. Graham never does, but this is of his choice, not mine. I think he enjoys the draft along the floor. At night he makes use, though sparingly, of his own bed in his own room. If this sounds as if I must be keeping him in luxury, that isn't strictly true. The room is there, and it would be wasted if he did not occupy it. The single bed was big enough for him and me when I brought him home as a small puppy. But when he attained his full collie growth it became necessary to allow for it in some way. I bought a three-quarter size bed for a front bedroom, thinking that Graham would join me there, but he chose to stay in his own room, and I was the one who moved out.

Ellie is not always with us but is always welcome. She is a few months older than Graham, and when they played together on the beach as puppies, I was concerned lest she be too rough for him. Now he is at least a size and a half bigger than Ellie, and when they play together it's mostly a matter of speed. She is among the fastest creatures on four legs, or seems so.

In the first years of her life Ellie vacationed on the Vineyard and spent winters with her family in Dedham.

Then the family moved to a house on a main highway near Philadelphia, a location dangerous for any dog, and even more so for one of her heedless temperament. About that time she went with Edie and me for a long walk in the North Tisbury woods, where she raced like the wind, stopping only to cool off in swamps, covering unimaginable distances, and getting back too late to catch the departing ferry. She has been on the Island ever since, dividing her time between Edie Blake's house, her official residence, and mine. I think we both enjoy the illusion of having two dogs, and Graham is delighted by the added companionship.

Ellie likes to lie on a couch. She lies on mine when she chooses, causing no damage worth the name, though I will not deny a certain downgrading that I charge off against the pleasure of her company.

No one has yet declined to occupy any piece of my furniture on account of his or her good pants, though some guests have hesitated, and others, tight-lipped, have pretty obviously made a point of sacrificing an important fastidiousness to an even more important standard of good manners. There has been some ostentatious brushing off of dog hair in the front hall, always ignored by myself. A fact of life deserves to stand by itself. Graham's hair, the rough hair or the fluff, is likely to turn up almost anywhere, especially in the long season of shedding. Graham is that odd-season type, a summer-coated collie, and is pretty free about changes in his coat.

The condition of one's house is always a challenge. The custom in Tudor England by which the king and nobles moved from castle to castle — if they really did — always leaving one to "sweeten" for a while, must have been an ideal solution. "Sweetening" would have been more efficient than housecleaning, and a lot less trouble. It can't be practiced now, because even nobles would run out of castles, and the socially minded are already worrying about the increase in what they call "second homes," a term that disguises a reality of these times.

Neither to my dog nor to myself would I say, "Grow old along with me," but in effect I would say it to my house over and over again. The joy of familiarity requires intimacy, wear, usage, and the accumulation of memories. That new rug in the dining room is a constant worry; only after it is stained will it be off one's mind. The companionship of a house is nourished by mellowing and shabbiness; otherwise you must always be on your guard, must never drop anything on the floor, must never put your feet up, and must eye your guests while they eat their soup, lest they score a miss with the spoon between soup plate and lips. Stuffing coming out of a chair is nothing to worry about unless it makes too big a bulge. You save money by leaving it as it is. To make things last was one of the admonitions of my forebears, and in this, at least, I can be true to their teaching and yet feel free to depart from it at times. If your average is good on following old precepts, you are doing as well as could be expected.

One notices a demand for old-fashioned things but not for the oldness of things, nor for oldness itself as an intrinsic value. The years have not been selective, and I doubt if people in search of antiques can tell when they are on or off the track. I happen to like toothmarks on my old things, and I choose to perpetuate associations with Graham and his predecessors that have enriched my life and tend to prolong it.

I was young once and can regard the memory with in-difference. Some scenes come back to me like slides shown on a screen, and that is a category in which they belong. I would not like to be young again, having had the best of it in those sunny years just after the turn of the century, but I would wish my dog to be returned to puppyhood over and over, with the same uncertain gait (trying to walk with his legs crossed, as Graham did), brightness of eye, fluffi-ness of coat, and inclination to try his needle-sharp teeth on the furniture. What does one want of furniture — value on the secondhand market, or a record of years lived without stint or grudge and always with an echo of laughter?

The remarkable imprints of Graham's teeth are not on a chair leg but on the corner of the baseboard near the kitchen floor at the entrance to the dining room. The wood is as frayed as shredded wheat. I don't see how he man-aged to chew into the flatness of those boards, especially without being seen or stumbled over. Perhaps he know-ingly did this, chewing while we were at the movies. At any rate I know why he did it. Obviously he did it because it was there. Other woodwork was there also, but this was more Everest-like.

I bought some deterrent fluid to protect the skirt of a large armchair that had taken Graham's fancy. The smell was vaguely of damaged lemons, said to be offensive to dogs. I sprayed the liquid as directed, not on the skirt of the chair itself but on loose rags carefully identified with the skirt. The deterrent did work, though inversely, be-cause Graham chewed the rags and left the skirt of the chair alone.

Large houses, when I was young, were referred to as "mansions," a title of respect that recognized both tradition and family prominence. The *Gazette* once had an unwritten rule by which all houses on North Water Street were to be referred to as "mansions," a deference to the manner and quality of the street's seafaring past. North Water was by all odds the most distinguished street we had.

One city man who bought a house on one of the prominent corners protested vehemently when he read in the *Gazette* that he had acquired a mansion. He suspected that mansions were taxed higher than houses, which is true, but a shrewd assessor will recognize a mansion no matter what you call it. Years later I spent a week in this particular habitation, house-sitting for a parrot named Coco, and I could see that the city man was right. The wind howled in the chimney, the third floor rattled and creaked, the staircase roared with peculiar downdrafts around its staggered landings, all of which fitted the literary character of a mansion but not a realistic one. My week turned into a sort of camping out.

The distinction I make as to houses follows a line between those made to be lived in and those intended to be looked at. The latter have the greater modern glory and shape the image in illustrated magazines.

The other day I leafed through a catalogue of delightful gifts and furnishings for a modern house, one of which was "a small bouquet of hand-beaded lilies of the valley in a clear acrylic pot, an appealing touch of spring. Imported from France, 5' tall, #5153-A, $25; shipping cost $1.25." That's not cheap for a gimcrack to be knocked off an end table by the tail plume of an active collie. It also cheats one of the fragrances of spring, and I am reminded to go to North Tisbury where some roots from my Aunt Adeline have flourished since she gave them to us long ago, and to pick the natural lilies of the valley, spring fragrance and all, from under the shelter of the bayberry bushes. Graham can make this pilgrimage with me.

How many knickknacks are on my mantel already? It is, I am told by Edie Blake, a Victorian slum area. Yes, but the accumulation is of and for memory, not priced at all in any marketplace.

In old houses I have known, the mantel has held a full-rigged ship in a bottle, a button from a Civil War uniform, a fragment of walnut wood from the wreck of the steamer *City of Columbus*, a cut-out silhouette of Aunt Meribah from the Philadelphia Exposition — things such as that. My own mantel display includes a headless china equestrian doll dug up years ago in the back yard, a stinkwood tortoise bought in 1937 at Livingston near the brink of Victoria Falls, two green lacquered vases inherited but provenance unknown, a china seal presented by the Audubon Society, a whale's tooth scrimshaw by a neighbor with the grape design of the *Vineyard Gazette*, and two drooping green plants, the name of which I forget.

I am aware of a tone of fondness as I tell of these, and they are to be lived with, not admired or commended to the appreciation of strangers. Storied knickknacks are in a category by themselves and do not crave embellishment.

Ralph Waldo Emerson wrote long ago: "I think it plain that the voice of communities and ages, 'Give us wealth and the good household shall exist' is vicious and leaves the whole difficulty unsolved." Eloquence follows, of course, and then: "The ornament of a house is the friends who frequent it." He left out dogs, a serious omission. "I do not undervalue the fine instruction which pictures give. But I think the public museum in each town will one day

relieve the private home of owning and exhibiting them."
He looked to the champion "who shall bravely and grace-
fully subdue this Gorgon of Convention and Fashion . . ."

The Gorgon, still unsubdued, turns out to be hydra-
headed, as proved over and over by the provocations of television and of mail-order catalogues, not the old-style Sears
Roebuck type, but the new and slick ones proliferating
with bright pictures. The postindustrial society is one of
advantaged living, possibilities unlimited, and it is not
restful for us who recall even better times.

Thoreau wrote: "In order that a house and grounds may
be picturesque and interesting in the highest degree, they
must suggest the idea of necessity, proving the devotion of
the builder, not the luxury. We need to see the honest and
naked life here and there protruding . . . The gentleman
whose purse is always full, who can meet all demands,
though he employs the most famous artists can never make
a very interesting seat. He does not carve from near
enough the bone. No man is rich enough to keep a poet in
his pay."

I favor pictures, a rotation of them if not too much trouble, each beloved in its turn, and poets will not be scared
off. The real ones never come for pay, and they usually
incline toward houses in which a dog gnaws the chair legs
and occasionally throws up on the living room rug. In a
pinch a man can be his own poet, unsuspected by the
neighbors.

Emerson was misled in his essay on "Domestic Life" by
adulation of children in the home. They are, after all,
messier than dogs. But Emerson wrote: "And so by beautiful traits, which without art seem the masterpiece of wisdom, provoking the love that watches and educates him, the

little pilgrim prosecutes his journey through Nature which he has thus gaily begun. He grows up the ornament and the joy of the house, which rings with his rosy boyhood." How the little pilgrim could find the ultimate companionship without a dog is a puzzle, and for a house to ring with glee it should have the obbligato of wholesome bark.

I remember a house at 87 Campbell Street in New Bedford and a small boy sitting on the front steps with a chocolate-colored cocker spaniel beside him. Along came a stranger dressed in the mode of the time, derby hat, fawn-colored coat with brown velvet collar, polished shoes. He accosted the boy in a how-are-you-little-man voice, though what he actually said was, "Hello, Commodore."

"Hello, Horse Manure," replied the little pilgrim. The cocker spaniel uttered a short bark of appreciation, and the boy put one arm around the dog's neck.

If this sort of thing did not occur, how would our planet hold its course even to the year 2000? The little pilgrim of whom I write grew up to be a lieutenant general, proving the sturdy health of the good old times some of us so well recall.

∽

A member of the Conservation Law Foundation tells me about South Meadow Brook, situated in the town of Newton. Under the Wetlands Protection Act and the DEQE, the brook has become a remnant.

"It is now a series of culverts adjacent to asphalted parking lots, underground drains, and piped diversions," my friend writes. "I 'discovered' South Meadow Brook when a mysterious oil spill appeared in the Charles River. Detective work traced the spill back to a misdelivery of fuel oil into the drain of a Newton gasoline station. By a circuitous series of underground drains, culverts, and even a hundred feet of surface brook, the oil had reached the Charles River. Much to my amazement this area was listed on the U.S. Geologic Survey map as South Meadow Brook, intact in some geographical sense as a little blue line running into the Charles River."

I did not find this encouraging to our Harbor View wetland case, which was still in the doldrums. Jerry Healy had sent a draft statement of facts, intended to be an agreed statement, but I knew of no word from the other side, and assumed that its facts were in some way different. Jerry's draft was pretty dry reading, and I guessed there might be some competition in dryness.

Unexpectedly, an opportunity came to meet David Standley, commissioner of the DEQE. I think his visit to the Island came about at least partly because of an article I had written for *Yankee* magazine about the Harbor View wetland case. I went with Doug Cabral, managing editor of the *Gazette*, for lunch with Mr. Standley at the Harborside Bar and Grill, where Dun Gifford had met the angry public officials at the time of the Kennedy Bill.

We liked Mr. Standley, who was not the routine type of Massachusetts political appointee and probably was chosen for nonpolitical reasons. I realized the inappropriateness of the blunt things I had been planning to say. I couldn't help saying some of them — they arose out of strong feeling — but at the same time I felt disarmed. I didn't know what he thought of the Wetlands Protection Act and didn't like to inquire.

There was a certain constraint, but the lunch went well enough, I thought. Mr. Standley was courteous, and later he viewed the site at Starbuck's Neck and I think he used the phrase "matter of judgment." There was nothing to complain about as to that, but we were still deadlocked with the law and its arbitrary standards.

～

I had decided to write as well as I could a chronicle of an uneventful day. The words "chronicle" and "uneventful" quarrel with each other, and that of course was the nub of my idea.

The earliest sound in Sheriff's Lane yesterday morning was the squeaking of my back gate. At this time of year Graham and I start our walk to the lighthouse in early gray light quite a while before sunrise. The squeak of the gate reaches out like a coarse whisper into the darkness. In my boyhood a man in New Bedford said he wished people wouldn't whisper under his sleeping porch. It was all right for them to talk naturally, but whispering woke him up.

Our squeak is not much in daytime, but before dawn it implies, or even states, a kind of imperative not unlike that of the angelus I used to hear from the stone tower of St. Lawrence Church in New Bedford or the whistle at the gates of the Wamsutta Mill. Early morning sounds always seem to mean something. They involve an alert. Of the lot I think country sounds are by all odds best, including that squeak of my back gate. When we contracted with Sonny Norton, he said it would be an old-time farm gate, and so it is. He did not guarantee a squeak, but we expected one sooner or later, along with the crankiness that accumulates with age.

A few summers ago a Sheriff's Lane neighbor spoke to me about the squeak. I said I would oil the hinges.

"No," he said, "please don't. I like to hear it when I turn over in bed in the early morning."

I knew what he meant, so I kept the squeak intact, hoping that other neighbors would feel as this one did, and that he would always be of the same mind.

Graham and I went slowly along the thickly shaded stretch of path near the edge of Sheriff's Meadow Pond, though we both know the path well. What cannot be foreseen is the way stones and roots rise up in odd places where all was level last night.

Two rabbits scampered over the tennis courts as we went by, but Graham ignored them, opting for his favorite shortcut to Ox Pond Meadow, under fences, through pine woods, until he would rejoin me at the turn of the road. The sky brightened, giving the shapely thickets and tall, waving grasses of the meadow a spectral effect. Milkweed pods by the random dozen swung in the frail breeze, almost ready to scatter their bursting floss. On the far side of the meadow, reaching almost to the salt marshes, a natural hedge of white asters stood thickly clustered to a height of four or five feet.

Beyond the meadow we met the pretty girl and her young yellow Lab, who are also early walkers.

"We're both earlier than usual," I said.

"Yes, we are. I'm glad you found Graham."

It was really Graham who found me. Day before yesterday he chose his own route home. He does this rarely and brags about it afterward.

On the lighthouse causeway I recognized Jamie Huxford by his voice because he was silhouetted, shadowlike, against the presunrise glow. He is now of middle years, though I knew him as a schoolboy. He was fishing off the lighthouse beach.

He asked me if I knew the whereabouts of his Aunt Caroline's journal. She kept it on a voyage she made with her husband to New Zealand, and I had read it years ago. In 1830 or thereabout, she and her whaling captain husband built a house at Orange Bay, Bay of Islands in the north island of New Zealand. Jamie said he hoped to make a trip to New Zealand in the spring. There was not only the story of his Aunt Caroline, but he himself had been at one of the South Pacific islands in World War II. He mentioned, though, an experience with cancer and said it had showed itself again and he would have to see what the magicians in Boston would do.

The sun had risen when Graham and I reached home. As I entered the house the telephone was ringing. A young girl's voice asked, "Is Cliff there?" I said I was afraid she had the wrong number. "Sorry," she said.

I needed one more editorial for the week's issue of the *Vineyard Gazette*, so I turned on the electric typewriter and wrote about Ox Pond Meadow, the milkweed pods, and that great hedge of white asters. Accompanied by Graham, I walked to the office with the editorial, saluting our friends the streetcleaners in their big truck as they went past. Years ago the streets were swept by Link Maury with a broad, stiff-bristled broom and a hand truck, two wheels, old style, on the front of which someone had painted "Caution — Power Brakes."

I settled again in my workroom upstairs and turned on the electric typewriter, but there wasn't much time left before an appointment I had made with a poet, Dan Smythe, who was for many years poet-in-residence at Bradley University in Peoria. Dan usually comes to our Island in summer, so I asked him what he was doing here in rather late fall.

"Writing poems," he said.

I had typed and discarded several fractional pages of copy when Dan and his wife arrived, greeted noisily at the back gate by Graham. It is simpler for visitors to find the back gate than the front one, though this means ushering them past the mowers, garden tools, old bottles and cans waiting to be recycled, and so on, then through the kitchen, dining room, and hall to the living room. The Smythes made this passage more easily than most of my callers. Dan sat down near the fireplace and disappeared from view beneath Graham's enthusiastic welcome. There's a lot of Graham when he makes one of his friendly assaults, what with his overall length, weight, and thick, rough collie coat.

"He won't hurt you," Mrs. Smythe said.

"Then why is he growling?"

Oh, Poet, I thought, who hears so many rhythms of earth and heaven, of ages past and to come, how can you misinterpret this variorum of a dog's pleasure?

"He'll settle down," I said, and soon he did.

Beginning our interview, Dan took out a notebook to consult as to questions he might ask. "This first one is personal," he said. "You needn't answer unless you wish. How old are you?"

I said I would be eighty-one in a week. Dan said to his wife, "Now you ask a question, Ruth. We'll alternate."

Ruth asked my wife's first name, and when I said it had been Elizabeth she recalled many happy associations with the Elizabeths she had known.

But the questioning languished. Soon, after I had been photographed at the back gate, Dan and Ruth drove off. I wonder how many of my contemporaries, if any of them, have been interviewed for the private journal of a poet?

One of Dan's figures has stayed fresh in my memory, for he was expressing the hour of a sunny Martha's Vineyard dawn "swirled over with heartbeats — pines and bayberries, / aspens, chewinks, chickadees /

> and the morning-webbed
> handkerchief of the Lord."

The image came back to me from boyhood when I would go out of doors early to see the dew-soaked gossamer whiteness of the grass with webs of spiders reaching all the way to the woods or the knoll or the stone wall where I took the path, barefoot, to fetch the milk. So like an outspread handkerchief of the Lord, but I never thought of it then.

I went back upstairs and turned on the electric typewriter, but right away the telephone rang again. It was Phyllis at the bank saying that the "call" report was ready for the directors of the *Gazette* to sign. This is the periodic statement or report the comptroller of the currency calls for on short notice, and it must be published. I didn't much mind the interruption, realizing also that it was about time for me to go to the post office. Going to the post office is a privilege we have. We need not wait for someone to bring us our mail.

All my life it has seemed a shifty sort of thing to walk past the tellers in a bank, pushing on into the severe, aseptic mystery of where Money is kept, counted, and handled. When I do this I always feel furtive. How does anyone know what I am up to? How do I know what eyes are on me or ought to be on me, with what dark suspicions? There were six copies of the report on Jan Place's desk, one more than in years past. No other director had been in ahead of me, and I signed on the top line, feeling presumptuous.

At the post office the mail had not yet been distributed and wouldn't be for a while. The postal service had cut down again on the allowance for clerical hire.

I walked to the newspaper store for my *New York Times*, and midway of Summer Street met Ruth Gordon, not a visiting celebrity of the expected sort but one who belonged to the Edgartown scene in her childhood. We stopped and talked a little.

Ruth reads in bed. She said that last night she had been reading the Bible and came to this passage: "And the Pharisees said to him, Behold, why do they on the Sabbath day that which is not lawful? . . . And he said to them, The Sabbath was made for man and not man for the Sabbath."

"Isn't that great?" Ruth asked.

I said yes, it was. Ruth asked if I had read E. B. White's letters, and I said not yet. Just then a man came across the street from the old telephone office and inquired if she was Ruth Gordon. She said she was and shook hands cordially. He said he had read her "autobiography . . . or biography."

"My autobiography."

He said he had enjoyed it, and he would tell his wife about meeting her. She smiled and said, "Thank you for reading my autobiography." He went back across the street, and Ruth said she didn't think E. B. White should have tried to "explain" Thoreau. That had stopped her because she didn't want Thoreau "explained" by anyone.

"You're younger than I am," she said, "and I'll give you some good advice . . . don't try to explain things when all the importance is in *feeling*." Then, as we parted, she said, "Good-by, Junior."

I am eight days younger than Ruth Gordon.

There was a lot of warmth in the autumn air, for the sun had risen just right to be looking at us directly. Autumn mornings in their own way can often get much the better of summer. I had even been inclined to go for a swim on a sheltered beach on the harbor, but had been put off by remembering that the breeze would be onshore and cool. I walked directly home with my *New York Times*, left it in the kitchen, and mounted the stairs to turn on the electric typewriter.

Really, though, it was time for lunch, or near enough, and I felt hungry. I descended to the kitchen, made scrambled eggs, toast, and tea, consuming it at leisure while I read the paper and Graham lay by my chair. Then I sat down in the living room to finish the *Times* and woke up about forty minutes later. The sun streamed so warmly into the room that I thought I would go for a swim after all.

In summer you are sure the water will be warm, but it never is *that* warm. In October you know it will be cold, and the cold you anticipate, though realized, is never, or seldom, enough to mitigate the zest, the ineffable October zest experienced. This is what you have looked forward to, but it comes as a surprise nevertheless, turning the swim and the memory of the swim into a delight. Graham and I had the sunny beach to ourselves. He hardly waded in at all, barking at me as I waded out waist-deep and plunged. A dozen or so strokes were enough. I emerged in a fine glow and said to myself that I felt younger, but reflected at once that feeling younger is something that comes and goes — best not mention it even to oneself.

When I took the temperature of the water it turned out

to be 64 degrees, not cold, not even chilly except psychologically. I have been in often at 55 degrees, though not for long. Virginia Packard swims late in the fall and takes 300 strokes when I would be shivering and chattering after 20.

Back at home I answered the telephone again. A young girl's voice said, "Is Cliff there?"

"No, he isn't," I said. "You have the wrong number."

"Sorry," she said.

I went upstairs and turned on the electric typewriter. I sat down for a few minutes until it occurred to me that this would be a good time to balance my checkbook, something I had not done for quite a while. I worked at this chore, slowing down when it appeared that the bank's figures would be hopelessly at odds with mine. I was about to quit in frustration when the telephone gave me a face-saving reprieve. I picked up the instrument prepared to say that Cliff was not in, but this time the caller was Miss Faith Adams of Beacon Hill.

She and a friend, Miss Helen Barry, had been coming down in the cars from Boston, she said, quite a while ago. Miss Adams was almost ninety and I had seldom heard anyone of her generation speak of traveling by train. They came and went "in the cars." (Thoreau used this same expression in 1856 when he started for Brattleboro and, reaching Fitchburg, found that there would be a wait of three and a half hours for his connection. He wrote in his journal, "and so walked on, on the track, with shouldered valise . . . Took the cars again in Westminster.") Miss Adams and Miss Barry had seen a most unusual-appearing man who wore a black coat that came right down to his shoes. The coat had an astrakhan collar.

"Now, you wouldn't wear a coat with an astrakhan collar, would you?" Miss Adams asked me.

I said I certainly wouldn't, omitting to add that the opportunity had never been offered to me. She said the dark, odd-appearing stranger had continued to trouble her and her friend. They had seen him again later on the Middle Road on the Vineyard, and he had seemed to recognize them.

"We reported him to the State Department and he was shot as a spy in the Tower of London," Miss Adams said. But whether this had been in World War I or World War II she was uncertain, and she hoped I might help her. If the railroad service had been discontinued prior to World War II, then necessarily the encounters with the stranger must have taken place before that.

Miss Adams remarked that a letter addressed to the stranger by the late William J. Rotch of West Tisbury had been returned because the addressee had been shot as a spy in the Tower of London. There seemed to be an interesting gap here, but I knew that Squire Rotch had died in the 1930s, and this in itself would identify World War I as the correct war. I so informed Miss Adams, who was grateful.

By this time, I thought, the mail at the post office would have been distributed. I walked downtown with Graham on his leash and found an unusually large accumulation of junk mail. I took out three identical appeals from Ralph Nader, Public Citizen; two from Environmental Action; three from a missionary college in the South; and two catalogues from L. L. Bean. I found only one brochure from the Committee for an Effective Congress, but I had received three of the same last week. The novelty in the

batch was a plea from the Association for Voluntary Steril-
ization, which did not detain me long. Several pieces addressed to "Boxholder" shot into the already overflowing
wastebasket.

What took my attention particularly was the telephone
bill, which included two pages of itemized long-distance
charges, the second of these pages being wholly unfamiliar
to me by locale and number. As soon as Graham and I
reached home I dialed the business office in Falmouth. It
turned out that the first page of the itemized charges referred to my own telephone, 627-4407, and the second page
to someone else's number, 627-4408.

"They are all sent out by computer," the young woman
told me, referring to the bills, as if this accounted satis-
factorily for errors of any kind. I guessed she was right.
Computers are a modern wonder, the more so because they
have institutionalized our mistakes. They have no ac-
countability and are not to be blamed. Absolution is
granted while the sins are being committed, as in Daudet's
story of *The Elixir of Father Gaucher*.

I now decided not to sit down at the typewriter again. I
thought I might as well quit for the day.

I took Graham with me and we walked over to Ox Pond
Meadow, where I thought I might cut down one or two
of the unsightly dead pine trees that had been complained
about. I had sawed off a few small branches when Frank
Mello came along on his bicycle. He is four years older
than I am, and I have been seeing him and his bicycle for
more than half a century. He remarked that no one would
believe him if he said he had seen me cutting down trees.

"You ought to get someone else to do that," he said.
"That's not your line of work."

We stood in the fresh air and slanting sunlight, review-ing the history of Ox Pond Meadow and adjoining lands, both of us remembering back through years and genera-tions. I guessed that he was basically correct, and this was not my line of work, not any longer, anyway. We had quite a good talk before Frank wheeled smoothly away. I whis-tled for Graham, who was actually lying close by, and we walked home.

I decided to put the lawnmower away, thudding it down the cellar stairs one step at a time. The timeless, shut-away feeling of the cellar, together with the relics there always made me think of the flow of years. Against the far cement wall stood the five-gallon kerosene cans, long unused, webbed by spiders; nearer at hand the dismantled coal bin we built in World War II; the outmoded storm windows that no longer fitted anything, bemused with dust; the sagging couch from our earliest years of housekeeping; the paint cans that should have been thrown out long ago.

An uneventful day was almost over, like so many un-eventful days, and years too, and as I sat on the bottom step in this undisturbed silence down under, I felt recon-ciled to the little account they had been. The flow of years, eddying, catching bits of straw and chaff, trapped now and then in lazy pools, so little concerned with the mainstream and the currents and rapids out beyond, yet closer to the solid ground, closer to the bank.

I remembered a passage from William James: "The only thing we directly encounter, the only experience we con-cretely have, is our personal life." It runs as it will, mostly — if we are lucky — a succession of common and ordinary days.

This was, I knew even at the moment, an evasion, a beg-

ging off from what hangs in the distance, almost surely —
as so many prophets say — the prospect of catastrophe in
the year 2000. Well, call it a plea for the other side, the
self-persuading argument of the everyday.

I stirred myself to go upstairs because I remembered that
two women from Oklahoma had written that they hoped to
call on me and Graham this afternoon.

THERE ARE ALWAYS a number of oldest houses in New England neighborhoods, but very likely the William Vincent house on the Great Plain is the oldest among our own. Venerable, spare, lean, deserted, weathered almost to ruin, it is at last being moved into the busy center of town. The moving raises some questions, and I doubt if the old house can settle any of them.

The journey from the Great Plain to town is over a route well worn in history for houses as well as for inhabitants — migration early took this direction — but the case of the William Vincent house is different because it travels as a symbol and also as a messenger of a culture long put aside. Its new life and meaning must emerge in a business center struggling with modernism, weltering, one might say, in tourism, competition, and operations of profit. Even in winter, it may be, the town's attention can be distracted only momentarily by the passage of an oldest house. Where is today's profit in it? Well, of course, a tourist attraction.

The William Vincent house moves slowly on steel I-beams, towed by a beat-up work truck instead of by oxen, so usual in house-moving from the isolation of the Great Plain. Nevertheless its passage has enough literary and wistful significance to be compared (scaled down for the proportion of our annals) to the ride of Paul Revere, the mythical carrying of good news from Ghent to Aix, or the message to Garcia that finally got delivered. We must recall such precedents, for like most towns that have survived so long, more than three centuries in our case, there is need of fresh intelligence from somewhere, and why not from the past?

On a new site in the town's center, near the courthouse, near the pillared church with the clock tower, across from the town hall, upstreet a little from the busiest stores, the oldest house will memorialize its birthright values from the community of scattered houses out there on the expanse of level acres, solitary, bounded distantly by great pond and ocean, once a community possessed of church, schoolhouse, barns, forges, Sunday services, and midweek prayer meetings. The Great Plain people — "Plainies" some called them — were known for independence and self-sufficiency and were apt to be taller and stronger than people who lived in town.

The age of the Great Plain itself is millennial. When the final glacial ice melted from morainal hills far to the west and north, the meltwater streams carried a broad wash of sand to cover many square miles as it shelved into the sea. Rightly, the greater expanse, first called Will Lay's Plain after an early proprietor, should be known as Willie's Plain, as generations contracted it. A geologist has written that one "sees a great level stretch interrupted only by the remarkable channels in whose southern parts lie the large ponds that are so conspicuous on topographic maps. At its northern edge the plain has an elevation of a hundred feet, from which it slopes southward at the rate of 20 feet to the mile until it reaches the level."

This is accurate for Willie's Plain, but the region of the Great Plain reaching from the outskirts of our village to the ocean on the south and Edgartown Great Pond on the west, has no groove or ridge or wrinkle other than traces of wheel marks made by truck wagons that carted herring from the Mattakesset Creek in the spring of the year. Except for these, which tend to vanish, the land lies as flat and perfect as if by a determination of nature that it should be just so.

Here William Vincent built his house, perhaps as early as 1672. Records show that at about that time he was suing Peter Jackson for debt, and later he pressed a claim against four Indians who had "detained his share of a whale and its Blober."

When William died in 1697 at the age of seventy, he left in his estate "one Neck called Shockamakset adjoining to Quenomica and so running by marked trees on the north to Meshacket Neck, and straight down to the pond on the south; this Neck, Meadow and upland being 25 acres more or less, with two acres at Quenomica."

Quenomica is translated as "the long-fishing place," the "long fish" being eels; and Meshacket as "at the great house or enclosed place," carrying the suggestion that the Sachem of Nunnepog may have had his dwelling and palisaded enclosure here. The value of knowing this is to establish the fact that William Vincent derived by inheritance from the estate of Towantquatick, who had derived by inheritance from the estate of the final glacier. A vast continuity is represented by the William Vincent house as it comes to town, and nothing from it should be lost.

William's will left to his son Thomas "ten shillings to be paid within ten days after my burial if he demands it, then my will is, and I do give my son Thomas only one shilling to be paid at demand after the said ten days at any time within a hundred years after the date of my burial; and my reason for doing so and giving my son Thomas no more than this is, first, I have given him near forty pounds; besides, he my son Thomas hath not demeaned himself well towards me nor his mother to our sad great grief." The will is signed with "the mark of William Vincent."

One may surely form an opinion of what William was like. Standing in the loneliness of the Great Plain, one is even more steeped in the culture he represented, best not put into words but left to the sense of the winds and the eternal beat of the Atlantic surf, so neighborly here always.

The old house also helps: steep-roofed with low eaves and big central chimney, walls insulated with clay — a forgotten notion worth reviving, since the clay absorbed the heat when it was most needed and breathed it out when it wasn't; wood construction, no doubt from nearby lumber, all within thirty years of the coming of the English from Wiltshire, the county and region of Salisbury Plain, Stonehenge, and rivers Avon and Kennet.

There seems to be little agreement as to what "culture"

is, except that it is always at war with other cultures or with itself. Dr. Daniel Bell, social scientist, Harvard professor, author of *The Cultural Contradictions of Capitalism*, is precise in his definition: "Culture, for a society, group, or a person, is a continual process of sustaining an identity through the coherence gained by a consistent aesthetic point of view, and a style of life which exhibits these conceptions in the objects that adorn one's home and oneself and in the taste which expresses these points of sensibility, emotion and moral temper, and of the intelligence which seeks to order these feelings."

Joseph Wood Krutch long ago quoted the French term for American culture — "cocacolazation" — the aptness of which one cannot miss, it being one reason for all the broken bottles by the side of the road — any road. Someone else says that culture is "learned behavior," patterns acquired by conforming individuals. It is fearfully obvious that "conforming" is the significant word here.

Reflecting on mass culture, Ernest Van Den Haag of the New School for Social Research thinks that "high culture" should coexist with it, but "mass culture is manufactured according to the demands of the mass market, cultural issues being decided by a sort of universal suffrage, the majority view prevailing." No elitest nonsense here, and no need for literacy in the ninth grade.

In the light of any such examination, the culture of our Great Plain and its people seems at first glance lean and stark. But the seasonal round of life, and of lifetime, too, had a firm aesthetic and urchin side, both felt and expressed, interwoven with tasks of springtime, summer, fall, and winter, all merging with hindsight and foresight into an orchestration. Considering the context of the longer term, or lifetime, we have William Vincent's will as an example, and for springtime and poetry a choice of home-grown expressions that have come to us by word of mouth mostly from the nineteenth century, especially its latter half. Here are some lines from a native and anonymous poet, by way of illustration:

> To the south'ard of old Edgartown
>   Is a great and level plain
> Where several farmers may be found
>   Who toil the soil for gain;
> But most they looked in days of old
>   For the springtime cold and bleak
> When they dipped the red-roed herring
>   From the Mattakesset Creek.

Waiving further examination for the moment, one may ask whether the William Vincent house should risk a confrontation with present-day Edgartown. How much of its heritage can our oldest house bring to town, and with what prospect of influence or usefulness?

The transplantation of buildings has been strongly challenged by Ada Louise Huxtable, architectural authority of the *New York Times*, who opposes "piecemeal salvation that dismantles and moves buildings," saving architectural samples instead of cities. "Pious gestures are an empty substitute for preservation. No one needs architectural keepsakes." Well, it all depends, and here that challenging word "culture" rears itself again.

I recognize the wounded plaint of the metropolis, an urban voice, from a teeming civilization that has so much to throw away and is in such haste to do it. Both cultural and economic squanderings have become a habit and a vice. We must assume that our case is different, without being at all sure that we are right; but in any case we must feel some apprehension as to what may happen when the William Vincent house arrives in town.

The house had its first modern confrontation back in 1895, when Collis P. Huntington, president of the Southern Pacific Railroad, a leading transportation magnate of the world and a millionaire besides, boarded our now extinct narrow-gauge railroad for a trip from Cottage City to Edgartown. Cottage City was where the boats came in, and the tracks ran just above the beach, six miles to Edgartown. On the day of Mr. Huntington's arrival, the single passenger car was crowded and the old boy — he was then seventy-four — had to ride in the baggage car.

One of his first wishes was to drive out to Quenomica to see the birthplace of his mother, Elizabeth Vincent, descended from the first William through a second William, then Joseph, then Abner. She was born in 1790, married a Huntington, and lived with him in Connecticut, where Collis P. was born.

What the great railroad capitalist saw was the likeness of many early houses, no other dwelling near, just the broad reach of hayfields, clover, tilled land, rim of low oak woodland, and a horizon that seemed far because it was as far as the eye could see, and a vast sky above it. There is no record of what Mr. Huntington thought or of the impression he took away.

The situation is different today, the new more often than not, and increasingly, in an adversary relationship with the old, and the old seeming to have less and less relevance to the new.

The William Vincent house is now gone from Quenomica. I drove out this morning and realized that although the ancient site is vacant, there is a greater presence than before. Quenomica is filled with a prodigious loneliness and an isolation so complete that it almost seems to possess weight and substance. The oldest house has left this void, a gnawing absence, without any precedent even in the millennial pause after the melting of the glacial ice, since from a place where there had been nothing, nothing could be taken away. There were no marks of occupancy until the Indians came, and now there are the imprints and patches of raw earth where the house stood, the reminiscence of enclosed fields and yearly crops, the soundless echo of departure.

I hear that the movers have reached the turn on Upper Main Street, and sometime today will pull the house into the grounds of the Dr. Daniel Fisher House, where a foundation is prepared for it. Here it will be a tourist attraction, as some say with scorn and others with satisfaction. But what more than a tourist attraction?

The Dr. Daniel Fisher House is a mansion in the Federal style built in 1840 from profits made in sperm oil, whale oil, and spermaceti candles. So these two houses, graciously separated by green lawn and trees, will represent a sequence, a historic profile, perhaps a symbol of varied aspects. That, too, raises questions.

I have talked with Ann Baker, supervisor of the moving project, who is deeply skilled in the working knowledge of old houses, how and why they were built, their ways of life, and their meanings. She says a good deal depends upon what visitors see when the front door is opened for them, and this must be basically true. Doris Norton, born a Vincent on the Great Plain, plans to send some furnishings that will eloquently belong in the house and ought to help.

Yet to visitors saturated in the affluence of these late twentieth-century years and aware of the entitlements they may assume to be theirs, the William Vincent house may be too plainly naked for any recognition of the culture it represented. Some visitors, of course, will try to "relate" because that is a modern thing to do. In the matter of "relating," Collis P. Huntington in his time had an advantage because he had started life as a peddler and had sampled many kinds of working and living, before, on a summit almost beyond ambition, he brought about the completion of the first transcontinental railroad. From this high place he could look back clearly, and he did not lack understanding of what he saw.

The past will not command the present to turn back, and wouldn't if it could. That is not the way of things. The past inveterately looks ahead. Yet there are many students of our society who take the view expressed by one articulate professor: "the human and moral alternative to our present course" is the creation of "small-scale, simple, frugal, steady state societies."

This is good theory, but how likely of realization? The frugal, thrifty life of the Great Plain is separated from our contemporary good times not only by progress, the arrival of the postindustrial age, and all that, but by breaks in our old family lines. Our ancestors are often regarded as strange people, no matter if in some ways remarkable; and how much stranger the old people who were not our ancestors? There is not much of an appeal in emulating any of them.

As to visitors from off-Island, or "away," they will no doubt buy postcards of the William Vincent house and mail them here and there. I think — and this is perhaps mainly because I have lately had uneventful days on my mind — that the self-perpetuating character of these days makes them one of the greatest obstacles in the way of any alteration in our lives. They are the chiefest anodyne of all, the comfort and security that make us what we are. This must have been so in the age of William Vincent, though the shadow then fell on the other side of noon.

Yet it would be frightening if in this age of television, automobiles, computers, and so on, we were to have nothing left that was from the beginning and unarguably now is our own. Apart from family trees and all such matters, the William Vincent house will stand as exactly this, by the most genuine right of succession.

⌒

Graham took up an exaltation of loud barking until I went downstairs to see if he meant it seriously. He did not. He was announcing the arrival of Bob Baptiste, who had come to measure for a new gatepost at the house on the other side of Sheriff's Lane. I remarked to Bob that Graham had scared off the laundry driver and two servicemen last week, though Graham really wanted them to stay. Bob said it was foolish not to know about dogs. We stood for a few moments in the early summer air, talking about things.

I said a heavy ladder for two-story or roof work, an expensive modern type, had been lying in my yard since last fall. It belonged to Bob's employers. Two carpenters had brought it when they were to fix the leak around the posts of the widow's walk on my roof.

"Did they fix the leak?" Bob asked.

"No, but they moved it around and lowered its volume, depending on the direction of the wind."

Bob said he had fixed a leak of the same type in a roof on

a house at Tashmoo, but in that case the posts came down into the attic. I said mine did not come down through. Bob said he would take a look, and that he would report the presence of the ladder when he went back to the shop. I said that rather than go to a lot of expense I would have the widow's walk taken off altogether. Bob said it would be a pity to lose the fine view. He said he imagined you could see all the way across the Sound to the Cape. I said yes, you could, and on a clear day you could pick out the towers of the Cape Cod Canal bridge at Sagamore. Going up was a bit of trouble, though, what with the bent hinges on the skylight and so on, and I couldn't take visitors up on account of the view of the attic rubbish.

We talked a little longer while Bob told me about the success of a new medication for his arthritis. This was naturally of interest, as well as tying us in with past generations. When Bob came back to fix the gatepost I didn't happen to see him, but the ladder was gone. The leak was not.

Prompted by Bob's remarks about the view, I climbed the stairs to the attic and the ladder to the skylight, which yielded stubbornly while I pushed on up and through. In all the years since the house was built we had made little use of the widow's walk, though once we watched an eclipse there that we could have seen as well from the ground.

The last time the house was painted, the painters said the platform was "all gone." It wasn't all gone, but the planks were embossed and slendered down by the weather of many years. I tried to distribute my weight carefully, and made a point of not leaning on the rail. My back was toward town. What I looked out upon was the wide pros-

pect of Sheriff's Meadow Pond and the remoter blue waters, John Butler's Mud Hole, the Eel Pond, and Vineyard
Sound with the bare and bended arm of Massachusetts
beyond.

Sheriff's Meadow Pond had fulfilled the destiny for
which it was designed, that of an ice pond. The icehouse,
an immense, high-shouldered structure, its roofline sharp
against the sky, was the most conspicuous landmark on this
side of town for many years, though hardly rivaling the
Methodist Church on the other side.

At one end a lean-to had been built to shelter a horse
and an ice wagon, and close by stood a shack for the gasoline engine that powered a hoist to lift ice cakes up a
ladderlike ramp to the coldness and blackness inside. This
particular lift was the invention of Louis H. Pease, who
owned the pond, and he had it patented.

On winter mornings we would look out as soon as it was
daylight to see Mr. Pease, a frail, old-time figure, walking
faithfully to the pond to gauge how thickly it might have
frozen. In many a winter the pond did not freeze deeply
enough for ice to be stored for marketing. A really good
harvest, though, might mean a supply adequate for several years. One time, I remembered, when the pond yield
was exhausted, Mr. Pease had a schoonerload of ice
brought up from Maine, and it was discharged at the coal
wharf and trucked to the icehouse in Sheriff's Meadow.

After Mr. Pease died, his daughter, Grace Ward, took
over the business, one of the first women to manage such an
old, established enterprise of the town. She had her share of
her father's good sense and sustained the worth of her
position well, allowing herself sometimes the relaxation
of a sense of humor. She was, though, a worrier, especially
when it became touch-and-go in the dead of winter as to

whether a freeze could be trusted to stay on, or was likely to yield to a thaw.

A Mr. Rideout was then broadcasting weather reports from a Boston radio station, his predictions having profound country importance. Grace would telephone him every day, twice on some days, to learn what the outlook might be. Once Mr. Rideout said that a thaw was imminent. Grace's father had left her a list of experienced and reliable men whom she could employ for the cutting and stowing, and she had his old foreman. Time was so short that the ice would have to be cut at night, I think for the first time ever, and Grace called her working force. A cable was strung from the nearest utility pole across the fields to the shore of the pond, and as night came on the floodlights cast widening beams as far as the pines Louis Pease had planted for a windbreak on the far shore of the pond. A black-crowned night heron dropped its startled *quawk* as it flew overhead.

Grace stood in a fur coat known to us all, her hands behind her back, looking on and occasionally saying something quietly and anxiously. A few of us stayed as spectators, not too much minding the unbroken cold. We did not know it then, but that spectral night's work was the last ice cutting we were to see at Sheriff's Meadow Pond, for a succession of mild winters followed, and by that time electrical refrigeration had possessed the market.

When at last the icehouse was torn down, friends congratulated us, believing we must be delighted to have it removed from our view, but we were rueful instead. We would miss that gray colossus, a brooding overlord in its own domain, at home with gulls, heron, kingfishers, and swallows in summer.

Grace lived on in retirement in her small house near us,

and we arranged a signal by which she could call us if she
needed help. A special window shade either drawn or not
drawn was agreed upon for the purpose, but not Grace nor
Betty nor I could ever remember which position of the
shade meant a summons. The matter proved unimportant,
for Grace never needed help.

The meadow, only so called, for it was never genuinely
a meadow, would never be the same again. Lest it be lost
to us as a native territory, and lest the pond suffer some
developmental fate, Betty negotiated with Grace to buy the
pond and its borders, ten acres in all of land, marsh, and
water. It happened that I had just sold the magazine rights
to a book, *Once More the Thunderer*, for $7500, and this
was the price we paid to Grace and her joint heirs. There
was no haggling, and I reflected that the "visit" of a couple
of hours Betty and Grace had together on the occasion accounted in good part for our opportunity to buy the pond.

So it fell out that at the one moment in history at which
Sheriff's Meadow Pond could be bought for $7500, we were
possessed of $7500 to buy it. Then followed the apprecia-
tion of real-estate values and the inflation that would have
put it out of reach forever, but all this did not take place
in Grace's lifetime.

We had not thought of "doing" anything to or with the
pond, but only of saving it, and now the question of its
future became persistent. A man from the Massachusetts
Audubon Society argued for a nature preserve, an idea
also favored by others, for they said the region had estu-
arial and ecological importance. But none of the existing
conservation agencies could be responsible for a lot of
small, scattered sanctuaries. There must be an endowment,
which we could neither command nor expect to acquire.

Betty and I came to a resolve at the same time. I talked
with our friend Judge Arthur W. Davis at the courthouse.
He was judge of probate, old style, who used to walk down
Main Street with his hands in his pockets, and you could
recognize him as far as you could see him. He wrote away
to inquire about the best procedure, and on December 11,
1958, he sent a bill for legal services as follows:

To services forming charitable corporation	$75.00
To services writing deed	$10.00
To services recording deed	$ 5.00
	$90.00

The charter of the Sheriff's Meadow Foundation was
issued on April 2, 1959, and the foundation was notified
by the Internal Revenue Service on September 27, 1961, of
its tax-exempt status. Members of the *Gazette* staff helped
at the beginning, but except for them the foundation began
mainly as a family affair. However it changed rapidly.

Gifts of land by neighbors, a two-acre swamp, remaining segments of John Butler's Mud Hole, and several
adjacent margins were received into the sanctuary. We
made one more purchase, with borrowed funds, to reach
the boundary of Planting Field Way, historic route to the
first division of common lands in 1653, "beginning at the
pathe of the meadow over the ware, and so to Hannah
Mayhew's marsh only the Pasture and Hannah Mayhew is
to have the meadow that lies upon the Pasture's Neck."
The former holdings of Sheriff Pease had now been
rounded out.

The cost of maintaining the preserve came to about forty
dollars a year, mostly for fees required with the filing of
reports. This was only the cash outlay, for I kept the paths

trimmed and lengthened them a bit. Neighbors helped, also, very much including Trueman Place, and we had a natural museum that required none of the grooming of a park.

Louis Pease's screen of pine trees grew to maturity and died, as old pines do, in northeast gales or from an imported blight. I planted swamp maples on the far side of the pond for the sake of fall color and bird life. Where steeplebush blooms in late July and August is where the icehouse stood, and there are also markers of blue flag and sedge. A few abandoned timbers still remain, rotting into the ground.

The other day an Internal Revenue Service man came down from Boston to see what was going on, if anything, and to pass a tax-oriented judgment on the foundation. I guess that all foundations were being inspected.

The IRS man seemed an everyday sort, urban of course, but maybe with a bit of small town (modern) in his past. I thought him not much past thirty. He showed me his badge, and then we were off, afoot, on the path around the pond. I don't think he much regarded the view, even from the dike where one could see, in the words of an old Chappaquiddick Indian, "all God's creation and part of Chatham."

Presently the IRS agent was inquiring, "Why do you keep referring to this pond as 'the old ice pond'?"

"Because they used to cut ice here."

"Why?"

This was a stumper. We were caught, he and I, on the opposite banks of a civilization sharply divided by time. Talk of a sort might be easy enough, but genuine communication demands much more. How could I explain *why* they "used to cut ice" on Sheriff's Meadow Pond? Where to begin?

Many images can pass through one's mind when a companion waits for an answer and there are no relevant thoughts whatever to shape a reply. I found myself hearing the familiar phrases of winters past: "Made ice last night," "froze solid," the first denoting a frail coating of ice, as on a bird bath or bucket, the second signifying the firm grip of winter cold.

Old scenes shuffled in my mind. How expert they all were at cutting ice, Antone, who was foreman, Abbott Fisher, Willie Bell, all of them, and how knowing and exact in their technology. First the ice of the pond had to be "plowed" as they said, though the horse-drawn rig used for the purpose was not a plow. It sharply cut grooves the long way of the pond, marking out the divisions that would become ice cakes. A bright, sparkling chaff of ice followed the blade on either side.

Next came the long saws, special tools to be employed with special skill, to complete the divisions and separate the ice cakes. Then the men with pikes to pole the cakes to the foot of the incline, where grippers on a motor-propelled belt would engage them and lift them into the icehouse. The incline was not steep at first because the icehouse was almost empty, but the ramp would be raised by block and tackle as successive tiers were stowed inside, each tier well bedded with insulating hay or straw. The cakes from the nearest curve of the pond were cut and stowed first; then, as soon as a channel had been opened, those from the farthest reaches, so that the pikemen kept solid footing for themselves and gradually left open water behind them.

This I was remembering, but what would I say to my

IRS friend, whose growing up had missed so much of the natural world and its elementary processes? With desperate simplicity I told him that pond ice used to be the only ice, and that it was harvested in such ponds as Sheriff's Meadow. I added that American Ice was quoted on the New York Stock Exchange as recently as 1930, though this wouldn't sound very recent to him.

It didn't matter much what I said after the first sentence or two, for my friend had turned himself off. He may have reverted to other matters — such as his trip that morning by automobile and ferry, or whether you are allowed to claim the greater of (1) $35 exemption shown on line 6d, or (2) 2 percent of line 46 but not more than $180 ($90 if married, filing separately).

If his thoughts could wander, so could mine, and I remembered when the icehouse was torn down, and wild cherry trees and poison ivy laid their pattern of neglect and disuse over the historic industry of pond and meadow. I did not speak of this to my IRS friend, but I did tell him that nowadays when the ice is hard and smooth, the town young people turn out for skating and don't go home until the ebbing of twilight, and the air is alive with winter voices. He and I parted formally and amiably, and I have had no word from him since.

He is not alone in his generation. This afternoon I looked again, as I had looked before, for "icehouse" in *The American Heritage Dictionary*. It isn't there.

∽

I am asked how far it is by path around Sheriff's Meadow Pond, and I am not sure. My pedometer is mechanical and thoughtless; walking isn't. I don't range around as Graham does, but I am not held to any regularity of pace. My thoughts, even, are detours.

My idea is that when Thoreau wrote those famous words, "I have travelled a good deal in Concord" — part of a sentence, really — he had in mind no more than a literal meaning. After all, his "walk," as he called it, covered ten miles from his house in all directions, and required a lot of traveling. In his journal he had written: "I have travelled some in New England, especially in Concord, and I have found no enterprise on foot which it would not disgrace a man to take part in."

Thoreau's intention does not matter much, since the remark itself has covered greater distances than he ever did, but it is interesting how deftly a few words can promote a plain statement to profound reverberations for the ages. I do not choose to be profound or pretentious, but I would not be misleading about this matter of distance, either.

This pond is no Walden. You can't swim in it. The color of the water is usually amber or brown on account of the peat beds and muck, though it is often disguised by the reflection of the deep blue sky. The bottom is too muddy for wading, and there are snapping turtles with quick, angry jaws and moody eyes. Otters and muskrats are more at home than any human could be.

The sheriff for whom the meadow and pond were named was Isaiah Dunham Pease, son of an earlier Isaiah and nephew of Sprowell, Rumamah, Harrison, Jeremiah, Fortunatus, and Salathiel, names that carry with them the history and biography of old Edgartown. Isaiah took office as sheriff in 1822 and served until 1862, forty years during which his title took possession of the region.

In old days an annual draining of the pond kept the

water clear, and only once, in the hurricane of 1938, was it tainted by salt spray from beyond the dike. Now it is a wildlife pond properly containing moss, slime, and the general detritus of nature. You don't notice this much, but it's there.

To relate the walk around the pond to a modern context, I would say that it has approximately the duration of a coffee break, and this can be estimated as to distance by the pace of the walker. When Thoreau wrote, "as if you could kill time without injuring eternity," he did not foresee the modern coffee break that tends to make eternity more robust and healthy.

One sets out along the path as one steps aside for a cup of coffee, or perhaps more seriously, with Herman Melville's design of "driving off the spleen and regulating the circulation." The commitment is of course considerably less than Melville's, the scale and occasion smaller, but the spirit not necessarily slighter in a civilization as desperate as ours.

Scraggly pines, a wild apple tree, and a spread of wild cherry trees mark the turn of the path from Sheriff's Lane into the wildlife sanctuary. "Path" is a term preferred to "trail" because it could only have been a path that Mr. Andrade traveled years ago when he followed his cows to and from their grazing on the pond margins, and that Judge Abner L. Braley took as a shortcut from the court-house to his big house in the pines overlooking Eel Pond. City people talk of trails, country people speak of paths.

Graham ranges around a good deal, and I see his plume waving above the ferns and blueberry bushes. I have wondered why dogs were as completely ignored by Thoreau as his journal indicates. I am aware of only one mention of a

dog companion, this on March 15, 1853: "In the woods beyond Peter's we heard our dog, a large Newfoundland,
barking at something and, going forward, were amused to
see him barking while he retreated with fear at that black
oak with remarkable excrescence, which had been cut off
above it, leaving it like some misshapen idol about the
height of a man."

No name for this big Newfoundland dog? Strange omission for Thoreau, who identified and named everything
else. I name both Graham and Ellie, the setter, who shoots
off and ahead with the speed of a fair wind, and is seen
rising here and there in a white swoop as she bounds
through the tangles.

For a short distance the path runs along the top of an
earthen embankment built long ago to provide crossing
over the depression through which an old brook reached
the pond. One hardly notices the elevation now, for its sides
are overgrown, with bittersweet and Russian olive mainly,
rampant escapees from some proprietor of years past. In a
little way the path goes native through borders of red
cedars, viburnum, high bush blueberry, wild cherry, and
bushes I cannot name and whose anonymity I therefore
continue to respect.

Graham turns aside, and so do I, into a broad opening
that reaches to the edge of the pond, giving the widest of
views. From here, in season, we shall see wild blue flags
and steeplebush among the reeds, ferns, and sedge. Of
course when I turn aside, the pedometer does too, a diver-
sion to be allowed for in the measure of distance.

We regain the path and are soon at the bend where wild
cherry trees and native maples are tallest, allowing open
space beneath for a special kind of lush grass that bears at-

tractive tassels and for wild roses to flourish in. At one side is a lofty tulip tree I planted as a seedling long ago and forgot about until I happened to discover its magnificent height on a day of revelation.

We emerge now upon a man-made rampart and outlook, the ancient dike where miracles occur for one who observes directly instead of through the educated filtering of science. For instance, how can the white tower of the Methodist Church half a mile away on Main Street be reflected so handsomely in the mirror surface of the pond? Not always, but upon occasion. The height of the tower has something to do with this, but not everything. There is also a fresh current of air across the pond and dike, the Venturi effect, named for G. B. Venturi, 1746–1822, that provides a breeze here no matter how still the air elsewhere.

Far, far up in the thermals on a summer day we can see the gulls, crows, hawks, any or all of them at their chosen altitudes, soaring freely, effortlessly. We stand and look up in admiration and a wistfulness bordering on envy. The other day Graham and I were held up here also by a blue dragonfly, Columbia University color. Fragrances of wild rose, yarrow, or sweet pepperbush add their effects to summer days.

Were it not for the dike, the pond would run off and leave only a marsh at the inland end. But the pond is safely contained, running off sometimes into a channel that takes the overflow to John Butler's Mud Hole, then to Eel Pond, and finally to Vineyard Sound. Old deeds refer to the immediate outlying basin in such phrases as these: "a small pond sometimes called Butler's Mud Hole," "reserving the right to pass on foot and with vehicles . . . to the marsh, meadow and Mud Hole," "to the center of John Butler's Mud Hole." These references are well spread out across the years.

On one bitter winter day I looked out from the dike across the Mud Hole, in which the tide had broken a covering of thick ice. Up among the broken cakes came an otter with the longest eel I had ever imagined, let alone seen, and began playing with it, tossing it in the air, catching it, tossing it again. I watched for as long as I could endure the cold. All such events as this tend to lengthen the distance around Sheriff's Meadow Pond.

A morning or two ago Graham and I set out on our walk and saw the pond hardly at all, just the sense of it under a frail white reek contrived by the chill night air meeting the warm pond water. October is a great month for such reeking, appearing like smoke if one sees it at a distance. When we came back from the lighthouse the reek was gone, and the pond had plainly turned to milk. I didn't wait for the effect to vanish.

Beyond the dike the path twists among wild roses, elderberry bushes, a cattail stand off to the right, and Joe Pye weed on the left, turn and turn about. Seasonal interruptions are common and welcome: redwings, only briefly absent, back from the south before the end of February; peepers in April, song sparrows singing, kingfishers rattling across the pond. Once I observed two in a confusing back-and-forth rattle.

On a turn of this path was where Graham encountered a skunk one winter morning and escaped because the trajectory of the skunk could not follow him around the twists of the path. Graham was properly cautioned, all the same, and profited by the experience. Lately on several oc-

casions I have seen him and a handsome skunk sharing the
fair territory of Peter Jay Sharp's Starbuck's Neck lawn
with mutual forebearance, soon after sunup, neither paying heed to the other.

Now we come to the knoll, the elevation slight, the name
justified only by tradition. Here the dogs run in circles
among the tussock grasses of the old field and around the
later cedars and pines. There are spruces, too, which I got
as seedlings from the Conservation District many years
ago.

Over at the right, hidden by beach plum bushes, oaks,
and wild cherries, is the private swamp for birds and other
life of nature, given to the foundation by the Morton
Feareys some years ago. The swamp is private by nature,
on account of brambles, mud in season, poison ivy, and the
principle of human avoidance, which is sometimes as good
as a conservation easement. But a prospect across the
swamp is possible from a peephole in the native growth.

The path turns again beyond the knoll, passes the spot
where the Edgartown Water Company planned to drill a
well some fifty years ago, follows an aisle between borders
of swamp maple, sweet pepperbush, ferns, and native
roses, and emerges shortly in open territory at the inland
end of the pond. We have observed the long vista often,
but it is seldom the same, and it conveniently depicts the
course of the seasons.

The final stretch of path skirts a boggy head region of
the pond favored by muskrats, and where if one knows the
spot, wild cranberries can still be picked. On the right are
the tall, straight sugar maples I planted, with the intention of having them form an avenue for the path. I tend to
think in terms of avenues when trees are involved, but the

concept is about all there is. Anyway, the sugar maples have grown beautifully and are all gold when autumn comes.

A short distance more and we are back at the starting point. I hardly ever remember to look at the pedometer to see what it has registered, but my own notion is that the distance around the pond is about half a mile — plus or minus, as surveyors have it — or about the duration of a satisfactory coffee break.

WHEN WILLIAM VINCENT moved into the Quenomica house, the Island of Martha's Vineyard still belonged to the Province of New York. Boston was much nearer to Edgartown than New York, at least in miles, but at that period jurisdictions ran along the coast, and the sea formed the readiest highway. When Queens and Kings counties were named, the County of Dukes County had its christening in the same litter, with this precise redundancy that was to be continued through the centuries. When the charter of William and Mary came along in 1691, the County of Dukes County was shifted into the Province of Massachusetts Bay, and Simon Athearn of Tisbury was elected to serve in the legislature of the province.

There were a few years in which the Island sent no representative to Boston, for one reason or another, but after the state constitution was adopted in 1780 no further interruptions occurred, and Martha's Vineyard came into the twentieth century with a constitutional guarantee of separate representation. In 1967, following the modern one-man, one-vote rule, this guarantee was challenged in court action.

The Supreme Judicial Court of Massachusetts ruled, however, in 1968 that Martha's Vineyard and Nantucket were "two compact, contiguous districts whose borders conform to natural boundaries and whose right to representation antedates by nearly eighty years the First Continental Congress." As to the one-man, one-vote rule, the court said that the historic separate representation of the two islands "would affect control of the House by no more than a possible .66 percent."

But Massachusetts in the late twentieth century was shambling along with a House of unwieldy size — 240 members — and good-government forces mounted an effort continuing over several years to reduce this to more efficient proportions. A referendum vote carried a constitutional amendment under which House membership became 160, leaving the separate representation of the two Islands not only vulnerable but practically impossible. The Vineyard towns, nevertheless, had voted in favor of the amendment, looking to its logic and not to its ultimate result.

Facing at last the imminent loss of the separate seat the Island had held so long, all sorts of political devices were tried to see if the loss could be in some way prevented. When an all-Island selectmen's meeting in February 1977 found that the end of the road had been reached, beyond recourse, a Chilmark selectman said, "Well, then, there's nothing for us to do but secede from Massachusetts." He offered a secession motion, which was unanimously and enthusiastically adopted.

John Alley of Alley's general store at West Tisbury, a selectman of that town, telephoned the day's news to a Cape Cod radio station for which he is correspondent and mentioned, almost as if it were some legal commonplace, that the Island Selectmen's Association had voted for secession. The radio station came newly alive. John could hear the air waves crackling. The storm was up. I have great distaste for the word "media," so overworn in modern use — and so imprecise or inaccurate — but it was really "the media" that took up the secession story.

Presently a secession vote was proposed at a Chilmark town meeting. Everett Poole, scion of an old maritime family and town meeting moderator as well as selectman, adjured the Chilmark voters, "I hope that when the ayes are spoken tonight that voice will peel the gilt right off the State House dome. If a seat for the two Islands is lost, we have no recourse but to withdraw from the Commonwealth." There were 132 ayes to 12 nays.

Little Cuttyhunk, seat of the town of Gosnold, outpost of the Elizabeth Islands, voted to secede, with only two votes out of sixty-five dissenting. Nantucket joined the movement: 1725 for secession, 404 against. Edgartown fell into line, 213 for secession, 12 opposed. Oak Bluffs rode high on the tide, 573 to 286, and so it went, the air waves still crackling and the "news media" making daily reports and observations.

I asked Everett Poole afterward if, when he made his

original motion, he expected the sensational results that followed — and continued, not only week after week, but for months. Everett said he did, and there was an old-time Vineyard gleam in his eye. He knew, all right.

When I was asked to write of the secession movement at the height of the extravaganza, I said that Islanders regarded with delight, and in some instances with mortification, the nationwide antics they had touched off.

Inquire of an aroused Vineyarder — and he was aroused, no mistake about that — if secession wasn't a lot of foolery, and he might very likely reply, "Oh, yes," depending upon the state of his interest at the moment. Ask the same Vineyarder, or another, if he was in dead earnest about seceding from Massachusetts and he would say, and mean it, "The deadest earnest that ever was." Both answers were true, and sometimes one would be truer than the other, but how could anyone but another Vineyarder be sure?

In no time at all, John Alley, who combines a bearded image of statesmanship with a rollicking execution of its duties, was talking long-distance with the governor of Vermont, and in no time they were on a first-name basis. Governors of other states, Connecticut and New Hampshire, allowed that they might be interested in acquiring Martha's Vineyard.

"We ought to get out of Massachusetts," Everett Poole said, "and have some fun at the same time." Everett is young and articulate and can carry people with him.

There was nothing comic about some of the grievances of the two Islands. Even with representation they had been treated by the legislature as if they were offshore colonies to be exploited. Now that membership in the House was reduced, it was proposed to hitch them onto some fairly remote part of Cape Cod. This was unnatural, but logical in an academic way, and nobody could think of anything better.

Everett Poole sent Governor Snelling of Vermont some of his frozen quahaug chowder, a properly famous delicacy, and Governor Snelling sent Everett some Vermont maple syrup in return.

No one could say that the extravaganza, in which the "media" seemed determined the entire nation should participate, was an exercise in any sort of democracy or that it was related even distantly to any actual democratic process. What was it, then? I said, accurately, as I now think, that it was the best demonstration yet of what could be called bumper sticker dialectic.

The bumper stickers were exuberant examples of this American idiom and its art: "Secede!", "Secede Now!", "Free Martha's Vineyard," and so on. Some of them, faded and ragged, were still on automobile bumpers over two years later. Nantucket produced one of the fanciest:

IN OUR NEED
WE MUST SEA-CEDE
Nantucket Island

A confident good humor, sometimes a mockery, always a bluntness, characterized the bumper sticker display, and there followed in the same logic, if logic there was, a wordy Proclamation of Independence, a freedom anthem sung by a beautiful girl at the State House, and a display of newly designed flags on television. All this in good nature, nothing rowdy.

Terry McCarthy, the Vineyard's representative until 1979, last of the independent line that began with Simon

Athearn almost three centuries ago, found himself a natural leader of the procession and proved effective in youth, energy, and resourcefulness. He gradually took over the operating role.

If bumper stickers seemed to assert more than to argue, it was nevertheless true that they did both. They skipped over the premise and came out flat-footed with the conclusion. If pushed on the logic side, one could shift over a little into the kind of dialectic that in this case may be supposed to have made the bumper sticker campaign respectable. My dictionary told me that the word "dialectic" was used in different senses by Plato, Aristotle, Kant, and Hegel, not one of them a New Englander. But taken together they put the term in a free market to signify the craft of polemics or controversy, at which Vineyarders have always been pretty good.

To maintain the forensic ground asserted by the bumper stickers and their allied national show business, the Vineyard could point to the historic fact that it had sent its own agent, or ambassador, to London during the Revolution to negotiate reparations for 10,000 sheep and 120 oxen taken off in a raid by the British General Grey. Nathaniel Hawthorne noted this when he visited the Island in 1834, when memory of this independent ambassadorship was still fresh.

"A province which is indefensible in war," Hawthorne wrote, "cannot strictly be said to form an integral part of the country with which it is politically associated. It must always be allowed a degree of independence." There was no present contention that Martha's Vineyard and Nantucket could not be defended, though in World War II a neighbor of ours pointed out that the Edgartown water tower —

a conspicuous standpipe on Mill Hill — could easily be bombed by the enemy. This much aside, it was easy for the Islands to feel and to exhibit their old-time independence.

Having gained national attention, though with an issue made up of earnestness and tomfoolery in undetermined proportions, the Vineyarders became self-persuaded to dig up and examine all manner of grievances and to stir up all the bitterness that injustice invariably arouses. Was not Boston always the enemy of fairness and reason? Almost always, as we saw it. I happened to be annoyed by the secession buffoonery, but I could evoke the strongest of resentments and other emotions over the duplicity of the state Department of Environmental Quality Engineering.

The County of Dukes County had been for decades the lowest-income county in Massachusetts. The director of our Mental Health Center had reported, "The Islander earns less, pays higher living costs, and gets less help than the citizens of thirteen other Massachusetts counties." All rural places suffer in this strongly and selfishly urbanized state, but the Islands have suffered most.

In 1978, the year of our lost representation, our county budget exceeded a million dollars for the first time. We were required to provide a salary increase fund against increases mandated by the state, across the board. The clerk of our district court got $8471 for salary and expenses in 1972, and the state now raised the figure to $21,117, and the district court justice was increased from $11,000 to $30,000 because he was to be assigned to the Island nominally full time. Full time for any judge isn't much, as I have observed judicial procedure, although it is obviously a different kind of time from that familiar to the rest of us.

The New Bedford, Woods Hole, Martha's Vineyard and Nantucket Steamship Authority, state-instituted but for

which no state credit was pledged, ran up a deficit of a million dollars when travel patterns changed and travelers preferred to drive to Woods Hole for a forty-minute ferry crossing rather than board a boat at New Bedford for an hour-and-a-half passage. The influence of New Bedford at the State House carried enough weight to perpetuate this folly until the Islands raised a fund by public subscription for an independent engineering survey and a statewide lobbying campaign that finally managed to separate New Bedford from the authority.

These were matters that had concerned the *Vineyard Gazette* through the years. It might appear that we had not done well even with a representative of our own, but the odds against us were heavy and, as Everett Poole said, "No one can represent the Island who has not lived through the trials and tribulations that come with Island life." And no others could feel the conviction and passion that were part of our heritage.

How solidly we ourselves can be united is also an open question, for insularity has always bred differences of opinion and islanders have always been opinionated and stubborn. Some say that the old spirit faded out about the time of the end of World War II, but however this may be, everyone entered into the dialectic of the bumper stickers and thus seemed to fall into a mainland pattern. Bumper stickers, in a word, spoke to the national spirit.

Why there should have been all this widespread attentiveness is, nevertheless, difficult to explain. I wondered how many readers of newspapers and listeners to radio and television understood what the affair was all about. Not many, I guessed, except for a sense of insolent revolt against authority.

There was, of course, much talk about taxation without

representation, though a major share of Vineyard property taxes were paid by nonresidents who had no vote. In Chilmark four-fifths of the tax levy was paid by the unrepresented owners of property.

Something new seemed to turn up every day to command national attention. Rhode Island was heard from. Representative Hugh Moffett in Vermont introduced a graceful resolution concluding with this sentiment: "There is no reason the natives of the mountains, the land of milk and honey, and syrup, cannot dwell happily forever with the tidal tribes and gatherers of the cod." Mr. Moffett, a former staff member of *Time-Life*, excelled in humor of a literary sort. His other interest at the moment was the legalization of barber poles in Vermont, where they had been a casualty of an antibillboard law.

Two Nantucketers journeyed to New Hampshire and enjoyed a quiet luncheon and press conference with Governor Thomson, who then issued a sympathetic statement. I received a letter from Governor Thomson, but I was too busy to answer it and I have forgotten what it said.

Of a different mind on the Vineyard were some like Harold Montamat of Gay Head, who wrote a communication to the *Gazette* beginning: "Enough, in God's name — and the name of our forefathers whose memory we profane — of this largely yokel-witted, country bumpkin flight of lead-bellied whimsy into the depths of Island 'secession,' " and ending, "Let's get out of this one fast lest instead of the desired wet nurse to suckle us, the white-coated man with the butterfly net and supply of funny jackets with tie-bound sleeves gets to us first."

It was said that a stranger with camera and note pad went into Everett Poole's place looking for a "character" and got put out — fast.

The president of the Edgartown National Bank was introduced at a mainland gathering he had been invited to address, the chairman adding, "While Mr. Vose is here, perhaps he will tell us what this secession business is all about." Mr. Vose's stricken expression vetoed the idea, but members of the audience called out, "Yes, yes" and "We want to hear about it." Everyone wanted to hear about it.

There was, or might be, a legal basis for secession, if reliance were placed upon Article IV, Section 3, of the Constitution of the United States. This provides that "New states may be admitted by the Congress into this union; but no new state shall be formed or erected within the jurisdiction of any other state; nor any state be formed by the junction of two or more states, or parts of states, without the consent of the legislatures of the states concerned as well as of the Congress."

The first step, introduction of a secession bill in the Massachusetts legislature, was easy, and it was not necessary at the time to consider the heavy odds against its passage, approval by Congress and the president, and approval by such state as might be asked to receive the Vineyard or Nantucket or both.

Speculation as to the effect of secession upon daily life was vague. Massachusetts maintains offices of the Registry of Motor Vehicles on the Vineyard and Nantucket; would Vermont, for instance, do the same? What about state aid for our schools? Such questions might be tossed about, but answers were not necessary so long as the fun kept riding along.

In the end, of course, the Islands were attached to a Cape Cod district, and our Terry McCarthy won official status as a Martha's Vineyard advisor to the new representative. If any of our grievances were alleviated I never learned what they were, and the incidence of new grievances ran along about as usual.

❧

"Secession was a nice and righteous idea," wrote a subscriber to the *Gazette*. "But that petered out with apathy. And all we have are T-shirts to show for it. So now we have something we can all fight for, Islanders and immigrants as well. Say No to the Big Mac."

Many months had passed since the secession circus; we had even helped elect a representative who lived on Cape Cod and, we suspected, would give us no more than a few polite letters, an occasional smiling time of day, and a cozy visit just before the next primary campaign. This is the way of politics.

But when McDonald's of the golden arches, fast-food purveyor to the world, planned one of its establishments — the 5110th, according to the *New York Times* — on the Beach Road at Vineyard Haven, time seemed foreshortened, and it was as if we had stepped from one campaign to another. On Martha's Vineyard one tends to date things by storms, wrecks, and tribulations, and the time in between seems to get lost.

I had no idea that an account of the McDonald's affair would be in the nature of a documentary requiring a good many pages for adequate presentation. National interest developed with surprising rapidity, and detailed explanations were expected by all inquirers, of whom there were many. I did not at first suspect that there would be any affair. I wrote an editorial for the *Gazette* under the heading, "What We So Greatly Feared," and expected that McDonald's with its corporate wealth, power, and sheer weight would quickly get what it was after.

I myself, being insular by preference, and my television set having been out of order for almost twenty years, had never seen a McDonald's or any of its images, but its significance in American life had been represented to me in many ways, and I could now share in the sense of outrage at the thought of a McDonald's on Martha's Vineyard. Even though the outrage seemed general, I was first aware of its intensity during the conversation at a cocktail party on a Sunday afternoon in late October, time of ruddy beauty and bright days of slanting sunlight on our Island. For a little while I thought that such fighting spirit, even if heightened a bit by the good company and excellent cocktails, might somehow prevail. However, as I drove home from Vineyard Haven I found my original doubts intact. The last thing I could have supposed was that there would still be arriving letters of protest against the McDonald's project many months later in the flush of another June.

I learned quickly, though, that McDonald's had entered the folk imagery of America and ranked as a symbol not much below the Ford car, the Almighty Dollar, and the American Eagle. In the attitude of the Vineyard there was also something that recalled the Boston Tea Party, one of the most enduring of the symbols of New England.

Two communications reached the *Gazette* in time to appear in the first issue following the McDonald's announcement. Afterward it seemed to me remarkable that these, well reasoned and clearly expressed, should have provided so satisfactory a rationale for a campaign in which emotion and fustian were bound to be the dominant idiom.

"There is considerable irony," Peter Barry Chowka wrote, "in an off-Island fast-food franchise usurping the lease held by a quality natural food store in a building that was for two decades a co-op market. The potential tragedy of such a development — in economic, health, and social terms — demands immediate attention and action by both the public and elected officials."

The fact that this site was on the Beach Road, so named, might have suggested scenic surroundings, but these were actually well removed behind a growth of commercialism. As I remembered the neighborhood from boyhood, there had been the blacksmith shop of Prentiss Bodfish nearby, the red-painted "humane house" where the lifeboat of the Massachusetts Humane Society was kept, and the collapsed roof of an old car barn where it was said improper trysts took place. A short distance toward the turn of the Beach Road an uncle of mine by marriage had a junkyard, the same uncle who put on his letterhead "Anything to Make a Dollar" until my aunt made him take it off. But Captain Cromwell's junk was mostly anchors and other marine gear suited to the character of the port. The development of modern commercialism had occurred in comparatively recent years.

New buildings had crowded in, traffic had unimaginably increased, everyone seemed to be going somewhere else, and the Beach Road had surprisingly little relevance to the beach and the harbor. It was, though, far too good for a McDonald's, any way one looked at it.

The Tisbury Board of Health, out of an inevitable concern with septic systems and drainage at this low elevation, so little above high tide level in the harbor, had imposed a moratorium on further building in the entire region. But this moratorium did not deter either McDonald's or the seeker of its franchise, Edward F. Harrington, a former mayor of New Bedford.

Peter Barry Chowka continued in his letter with a portrait of McDonald's: ". . . a virtual international empire with 3000 restaurants and yearly sales that have increased more than twentyfold from $129 million in 1964 to $2.7 billion in 1976, and an annual advertising budget of more than $100 million; the chain is the largest single consumer of meat in the United States after the armed services and plans to open one new restaurant a day for the next decade."

These statistics would be updated, but they were sufficient for the time.

Former Mayor Harrington had said, "Our primary interest is in the people of the Island," a fatuous thing to say. "Who's he trying to kid?" asked Peter Chowka.

Peter, who was so prompt with a charter of liberty and declaration of hostilities, was young, lean, attractive, and an excellent writer. He had been living on the Vineyard for about six years, most recently in the green and open countryside of Lambert's Cove. He had gained experience in the George McGovern presidential campaign, had background in radio and showed professionalism in relations with the press. He had ideas about nutrition, and some might have called him a food faddist, a term I don't think he would have minded.

The second definitive opening letter in the *Gazette* came from David Frantz, a marine biologist who commuted back and forth from the scientific community at Woods Hole and was a contributor of good sense to public affairs of the Vineyard.

How many jobs would McDonald's bring to the Island? "Very few, I suspect," Mr. Frantz wrote. "The success of McDonald's is due in part to the efficiency with which they manage to serve their product. It is not a labor-intensive restaurant. Furthermore, if successful, it will seriously threaten the jobs and in fact the very businesses that now supply this particular market in a more acceptable way. Artcliff Diner, the bowling alley coffee shop, and others are in trouble with a successful McDonald's across the road. And the cash flow generated by all the businesses of this type will be increasingly off-Island . . .

"As for aesthetics, perhaps the character of the building will be preserved, but what of the paper plates? And if traffic (and its incremental cost to Vineyard Haven) can be considered as aesthetics, just how does Mr. Harrington reason that a drive-in hamburger establishment would possibly help? Our traffic problem on Beach Road Five Corners is bad enough now . . .

"But the most important objection to this proposal to me is simply the fact that if consummated, this project will signal the beginning of the end of Vineyard Haven as a superior town in which to live . . ."

In that same issue of the *Gazette*, Jack "Mervie" Schimmelman, as he signed himself, inserted a four-line classified advertisement inconspicuously headed, "Announcement," which read as follows: "Everyone interested in keeping McDonald's off-Island is invited to an ad-hoc group meeting at Grace Church, Monday, November 13, at 8:15 P.M." The response was astonishing. Some sixty people showed up, a turnout few of our major efforts succeed in attracting.

Mr. Schimmelman identified himself a little later when a proponent of McDonald's suggested that the opposition showed an upper-crust indifference to the welfare of the workingman.

"I am temporarily off-Island trying to earn some money (for a change)," he wrote. "I am thirty and have been working since I was eleven. I have done everything from cleaning employees' toilets in a hotel to teaching to directing a theater of my own. It hasn't been unusual for me to average sixty hours a week and/or seven days a week. In short, I know about working and being poor. It's just a fact of my life . . ."

Instead of settling for a diet of "sugar and fat and untold numbers of carcinogens" he went on, "The 'poor working people' (what an heroic title) . . . should assert a right to good nutrition . . . We must do away with the slave in our heads."

The McDonald's affair would proceed through a series of confrontations — an initial presentation of the formal application to the Tisbury Board of Health, the return a little later with an amended application, and a few peripheral skirmishes. But at the start, letters to the *Gazette* opposing McDonald's came in large volume, with varying degrees of ferocity and protest. It seemed to me that the letters were the leitmotif of action pursued by Peter Chowka and the No-Mac Committee. For many years I had thought that a "leitmotif" signified a theme on the light side. I had not caught up with the Wagnerian Association or followed "leiten" into the old German where it could be defined as "to lead" or "to go forth." The word now seemed appropriate. Or I might have invoked Christopher Morley's *Thunder on the Left*, a title derived from Sir Eustace Peachtree of the seventeenth century: "Among the notionable dictes of antique Rome was the fancy that when men heard thunder on the left the gods had something of special advertisement to impart. Then did the prudent pause and lay down their affairs to study what Jove intended."

"I am appalled and disheartened at the prospect of a McDonald's fast-food restaurant on the Beach Road," one letter began.

In different tone another: "Zounds! Egad! All these Clamshell Alliance and Anti-Nuke folks have something to sound off about now at the latest scourge to the Vineyard — a fast-food emporium . . ."

Another: "Just imagine a Pizza Hut replacing the old Harbor View Hotel . . . Howard Johnson's orange roof gracing Beetlebung Corner . . . Arthur Treacher's Fish and Chips on the waterfront at Lucy Vincent Beach . . . a Holiday Inn at Gay Head . . . Wendy's Hot 'n' Juicy just across the road from the Home Port . . . and that jolly old Burger King next to the Tabernacle in Trinity Park . . ."

Shortly after this there were letters sharing experiences elsewhere and offering good advice. Tennessee and Arizona were heard from. A physician in Philadelphia wrote: "I remember a time when the office building in which I work did not have a McDonald's next door, and there were no Styrofoam cups, napkins, sandwich containers, etc., messing up the place. Now, since McDonald's opened, it is a disgrace."

Of course there were contrary opinions. A writer reported that a study of the food value of McDonald's had found the foods "a lot better than detractors would have us to believe. But most important, McDonald's has become a cultural phenomenon which I don't think should be denied to Island residents . . . Like it or not, without a McDonald's our kids suffer a kind of cultural deprivation . . ."

An absentee Vineyarder stated an opposite view of the "highway culture" that "adds up to a dreary, spiritless sameness that we take for granted mile after mile and hour after hour of ceaseless and mind-killing boredom . . . And now to Martha's Vineyard comes Fast Food. The highway culture has spanned Vineyard Sound without the aid of a bridge . . ."

The poetic muse was not absent, expressing various degrees of mockery and humor, but without improving on the prose. Among the briefest communications were these:

"McDonald's? I can't believe it!" This from Chicago. "What if they opened a McDonald's and nobody came?" This from closer by.

The No-Mac Committee — the name seemed self-incubated — took on more definite form, though it never went through the formality of organizing and electing officers. The active group was led by Peter Barry Chowka, and it included a scholar of graphics, Don Newgren; a liaison with the advertising department of the *Vineyard Gazette*, Christine Powers; and a medical authority, Dr. Barry Marron of the National Institutes of Health at Bethesda, Maryland. From petitions and communications the committee now pressed its warm-up campaign to big-scale newspaper advertising: HELP STOP McDONALD'S — WRITE NOW.

Soon, the week's news story in the *Gazette* was headed BIG MAC CLOSING IN, and our editorial, at the suggestion of our managing editor, Douglas Cabral, appeared under the words NOT WANTED. The news story reported, "So far both sides are just eyeing each other, but a meeting of the two isn't far off."

McDonald's had something to say publicly for the first

time, through its corporate relations official, Douglas Timberlake, who stated, "Of course we listen to public opinion. In one community that comes to mind we met considerable community opposition and we withdrew. The site is now occupied by a porno movie house. It depends on whether the opposition is a broad basis of community displeasure. We provide what we consider to be a high-value service — a quality product with a good reputation, served in clean surroundings. When we see an area where there is need for the service we try to put the two together."

Peter Chowka was not impressed.

Mr. Harrington said, "If it were a complete residential area I would understand an argument that we were changing the character of the neighborhood. But we're talking about an area that is dedicated to commerce. I don't see that this business is different from any other. It is completely consistent with the prevailing mood of the area."

To a stranger, and Mr. Harrington was one, this view seemed reasonable, but to Vineyarders it was too much like Spiro Agnew on the subject of slums and Ronald Reagan on redwoods — "If you've seen one, you've seen 'em all." The Beach Road, though roughly treated, had a uniqueness that was the Vineyard's own.

At about this time, Erik Pfau, a member of the No-Mac Committee, called me to say he thought the committee ought to have names of community prominence in order to make an impression on McDonald's. Mr. Timberlake had certainly indicated that this was the case. Erik himself was retired from business, an all-year resident, and an acute critic in public affairs. The anti-Mac movement had been endorsed by the Garden Club, Friends of Tisbury, and the president of the Chamber of Commerce, but more seemed to be indicated.

I told Erik that in my experience the gentry, so called, or the leaders in the community, usually held back from such campaigns because of dignity or because they wanted to keep a low profile or did not want to stick their necks out. On my way home I mulled this over, remembering a pair of quotations I had long ago taken to heart. So I called Erik back to say that I would be glad to espouse this No-Mac cause but that I could not attend meetings.

Could not, or would not, it was all the same. The hour at which Graham and I got up in the morning, the stroke of five, put our day out of synchronism with that of most others. I was deeply involved in the Harbor View case, which made noises as if it were coming alive again, maybe with an early hearing in Boston. I was also writing three editorials a week for the *Gazette* and trying to finish a book of my own, to get to bed at night at a reasonable time, and to keep up what is often called an extensive correspondence. This meant, among other things, that I had to answer the people who wrote to me about such matters as genealogy, and there were a lot of them.

The next morning Erik telephoned to tell me I had been named honorary chairman of the committee. I suppose I was only momentarily surprised, and I certainly had no misgiving or regret. The first of the quotations I keep with me and that had bespoken themselves on my walk home was from Felix Frankfurter:

"What is it that makes so many men timid creatures? I can give myself some answers. People want to avoid unpleasantness. Life is hard enough even if you have a bank account . . . Why stick your neck out? That lovable invitation to do nothing."

The second came from C. P. Snow's novel, *The Affair*:

"Also I knew, and I knew this in the wreckage and

guilt of my life behind me, that there are always good, sound, human, sensible reasons for contracting out. There is great dignity in being a spectator; and if you do it for long enough, you are dead inside . . ."

Perhaps I had the best of two possible choices, for the others did the work and I became, at the cost of little effort, the center of a national vortex this campaign had set boiling. Peter Chowka brought in a *Boston Globe* staff man, Peter Anderson, in a round of interviewing and observation, and the *Globe* story was immensely helpful. Then came Chowka's professionally prepared releases, nicely timed. The wire services, UPI and AP, sent out stories that produced responses from all over the country.

A fully equipped television team was brought to my house by Peter Chowka for an interview that obviously carried far. Letters arrived from places as varied as Albuquerque; Villa Ridge, Missouri; Topeka; Sarasota; Babylon, New York; Minnetonka, Minnesota; Palatka, Florida; Pottersville, New Jersey; Bloomville, New York; Swansboro, North Carolina; Pittsburgh; Basking Ridge, New Jersey; Santa Barbara; Newburgh, New York; Churchville, Maryland; Edmonds, Washington; Honeoye Falls, New York; Wilmette, Illinois; Syracuse — all opposed to a Big Mac on Martha's Vineyard. Some said the writer would boycott McDonald's in his or her home town. Many letters, of course, came from seasonal visitors to the Vineyard, but an impressive number were from strangers and outsiders.

More of Don Newgren's novel advertising appeared in the *Gazette*, and then came the Tisbury Board of Health hearing at which the application of Mr. Harrington for the Beach Road location and a Big-Mac establishment was presented. The small quarters of the Board of Health, an annex of the town hall, accommodated a diverse crowd, as the *Gazette* reported, including "the young and the old, the staid and the silly, in all manner of dress." All seemed united in opposition to Big Mac.

Dr. Michael Jacobs, chairman of the Board of Health, pointed out that the Harrington application bore no professional engineer's stamp and no required certification that the system conformed to flood hazard requirements. It seemed to meet neither town nor state health codes. Dr. Jacobs also asked Mr. Harrington if he was aware of the moratorium against Beach Road building.

Mr. Harrington was aware of it but still wanted to meet with the Board of Health again as soon as possible with an amended application.

Said the *Gazette*: "The dialogue so far has not been particularly courteous on either side and shows no sign of moderating." "Sac the Mac," "Stop the Big Mac Attack," said the T-shirts and bumper stickers.

Erik Pfau explained to Mr. Harrington the background of all this opposition — essentially that the Vineyard is a special place. "Well, it won't be special long," responded Mr. Harrington.

That did it. Mr. Harrington's portrait appeared in the next big display advertisement in the *Gazette* with the quoted words, "It won't be special long." "Mr. Harrington," said the text, "and the McDonald's representatives have shown a cynical, arrogant contempt of the wishes of the community — but the tide of opposition continues to swell. We must see that McDonald's receives the message that they are not wanted ANYWHERE on Martha's Vineyard."

Our editorial remarked that "Mr. Harrington, former mayor of New Bedford, who is trying to get a foot in the door for a McDonald's establishment on the Beach Road in Vineyard Haven, did not come here in an official capacity, and therefore one cannot speak of his statesmanship, but his manners were terrible."

November 1978 had now run its course. The leaves that had rustled and turned color in October had long since been swept away in the windy advance of seasons. Darkness came early. Nights were chill, and Graham and I hedged a little on our time of getting up in the morning.

Peter Chowka added to the documentation of the Mc-Donald's affair with an interview that, although not immediately published, seemed to merit inclusion in some anthology of corporate attitudes. He wrote:

The Tisbury Board of Health meeting on December 11 gave us our first look at the McDonald's representatives. After the meeting I talked with Jack W. Ochtera, McDonald's real-estate manager for the northeast region. Our conversation was tape-recorded with his knowledge and significant transcribed portions that might interest people are reproduced here.

Q.: When did McDonald's first get interested in the Vineyard?

MR. OCHTERA: We've always been interested in the Island for years.

Q.: Why is now the time to come here?

MR. OCHTERA: Maybe availability.

Q.: One of your representatives was quoted in the *Vineyard Gazette* as saying that on occasions you back away from plans to go into a community. When do you reach that point, that you decide it's not worth it?

MR. OCHTERA: Let me say it wouldn't be because of the people who were here tonight.

q.: What about the [anti-McDonald's petition with] 1500 names that represent 20 percent of the Island's residents?

MR. OCHTERA: I wouldn't even consider it.

q.: What kinds of things do you consider?

MR. OCHTERA: Strictly internal. It would be a strictly internal decision.

q.: Both Mr. Harrington and a McDonald's official said in the *Gazette* that if there were a certain amount of opposition they might back off from the proposal. I'm wondering, do we have to sign up 50 percent of the Island's residents, or would that make a difference?

MR. OCHTERA: I don't think that's really a determining factor. If we walked away from every location where people have voiced objection to us we wouldn't have built 5000 restaurants.

q.: The moratorium [on Beach Road] — do you consider that an impediment?

MR. OCHTERA: It's an obstacle.

q.: Is there consideration on your part now for another location on the Island?

MR. OCHTERA: It could be.

q.: Are you in touch with any other chains, because we've heard that Burger King is targeting the Island now?

MR. OCHTERA: I know what you're saying — we come in and everybody follows. We know that happens and we don't like it either. If an area is zoned properly and we're permitted use, we have to go forward and make certain appeals and go for certain variances. If we feel it's beneficial to us, we do it, and if we don't think it is, then we reconsider and we do renege and walk away from a deal. We have certain obligations to our stockholders.

q.: Basically it's an economic question?

MR. OCHTERA: We have an aggressive growth plan and we try to meet that . . . We have rights like everybody else. If we're permitted use, and they [the authorities] are arbitrary and capricious and all those other words they throw around, then we pursue.

Q.: You pursue it?

MR. OCHTERA: As far as we have to.

Q.: Do you ever pursue it for the principle of the whole thing?

MR. OCHTERA: Yes, there's a possibility of that, too; sure, it's a possibility.

That phrase of Mr. Ochtera's — "the people who were here tonight" sounded slighting or derogatory. He might or might not have felt the same way about others on the anti-Mac list. *Variety*, which is interested in such matters, culled out a selection of names and printed it under the headline, "A Big Mac is Scarier Than Jaws to Chic Folk on Martha's Vineyard." The names included Robert Crichton, Mrs. Max Eastman, Mia Farrow, Ruth Gordon, E. Y. (Yip) Harburg, Garson Kanin, Vance Packard, theater director Mary Payne, radio commentator Duncan Mc-Donald, Jules Feiffer, author Anne Simon, James Taylor, Carly Simon, William Styron, and John Updike. I was included also, but *Variety* missed Beverly Sills.

The Tisbury Board of Health met again for a second major confrontation. Mr. Harrington had revised his application, and it was now in legal form. The board accepted it for consideration but stuck to its Beach Road moratorium, though a plan for another site remained possible.

Douglas Cabral's story in the *Gazette* quoted Mr. Ochtera from his office in Westwood, Massachusetts, as saying that the Islanders should not use the word "victory." From McDonald's point of view nothing had been lost because the chain itself had not asked for anything. It was Mr. Harrington who had filed the application, and it was he who had suffered the rebuff.

Mr. Timberlake, also quoted, said, "McDonald's was not specifically involved there. The building wasn't ours and we had no agreement with Harrington."

Mr. Ochtera went on, "So far as I am concerned, the whole thing was beaten to death." Of the national uproar he remarked, "It was a sleeping giant, a sensational thing. I had a call from Chicago [McDonald's corporate headquarters] and they wanted to know what the hell we were doing out here. Stockholders had called, wanting to know what was going on."

The *Gazette* story continued: "Mr. Timberlake was on the receiving end of a great deal of that noise in his Oak Brook office. He said Wednesday he'd received 75 or 100 letters from anti-Mac correspondents. 'It seems like a lot,' he said, 'but it's hard to tell. No one ever suggested that people write me before.' " McDonald's regularly expects some opposition to a plan to open a new outlet, but the campaign mounted by the No-Mac Committee broke form with all past experience.

The UPI dispatch began: "Martha's Vineyard officials have blocked a bid to plant the golden arches of McDonald's on this vacation island, but a spokesman for the restaurant said Wednesday he hadn't given up the Big Mac attack. The Board of Health, to the cheers of about 70 residents, Tuesday night rejected a revised plan for the proposed restaurant in this scenic town seven miles off the Massachusetts coast. However . . . a regional real-estate representative said Wednesday he was looking for another suitable site . . . 'It could be next week, it could be six months, it could be a year from now — whenever we find a site that's suitable we'll pick up the ball again.' "

The definitive story in the *New York Times*, headed, "Martha's Vineyard Repulses Big Mac," ended, I thought, on an elegiac note. "We felt it was a long shot, but you never know until you try," Jack Ochtera was quoted. ". . . But we will continue to consider alternate sites as they come up. If we can get in some place, then we have an obligation to our stockholders to do so. But we have other things to do here, and no one needs the aggravation of a Martha's Vineyard."

Every indication is that the aggravation will be resumed, on call, if occasion arises, with the experience of the No-Mac Committee to aid in its further exploitation.

For solace and meditation I went yesterday to the public library. This was originally a Carnegie library, built on a splendid North Water Street site given for the purpose by a remarkable woman of an old whaling family. Grace Allen remembered her.

"Here in New York there is rain," Grace once wrote to me, "and noise, plenty of both, and so I am escaping, walking down North Water Street in memory.

"Just before reaching the library is Mrs. Warren's house. She used to sit on the front porch, and I was a little bit in awe of her because she was so very dignified. She held her head tipped back so that she seemed to me very queenly, at least until the day that she asked me to come up to the porch steps, and patted my hand. I liked her very much, and in my mind's eye I still see her, head a bit tilted back, looking down at me. When I came to New York, still very young, I saw the magnificent stone lions guarding the public library at Fifth Avenue and 42nd Street, and the way they held their heads reminded me of Mrs. Warren."

I suppose our library is now modern, and it must strike many people that way, but to me it is timeless. The muted green of soft wall-to-wall carpeting, a silence gentle enough for satisfaction but not complete enough to be isolating, ceiling panels admitting unobtrusive light with the aid of an overhead louver, clean straight lines of doorways and windows — these are provisions of modernity, but admittance to this serenity is admittance to a seamlessly joined past. The books, so many of them, are all around in orderly stacks, with wide aisles and occasional tables and chairs among them.

I thought of the old library, lacking in depth and space as compared with this, and of the conspiratorial lady librarians who supervised our reading and kept dangerous or libidinous books under the front desk, for the use only of mature persons. These turned out to be an intimate group who whispered together over the really exciting scandals. This form of censorship had its convivial side, as I think censorship generally does in a vicarious way.

Now I followed an impulse to loiter. I came upon a copy of Henry Miller's *Tropic of Cancer* on an open shelf. It had not been in brisk circulation, no more frequently taken out than *Middlemarch*. I was pleased that *Middlemarch* had not been completely passed by in the new generation of readers.

I accepted the invitation of a corner chair and table, ignoring a sign that asked me not to put my feet on the table.

I am never comfortable when I do that, but apparently some people are. Easily within reach I saw *A Henry James Reader* and took it from the shelf. I had come rather late in life to a real liking for Henry James.

I riffled through the pages and came to "The Beast in the Jungle," which I began to read again. I like the way Henry James drops adverbs into his sentences as if with special relish: "He strangely found himself looking," "she consequently asked," "the girl mournfully sighed," "I only knew what inadvertently I oughtn't."

Leon Edel, editor of the book I held in my hands, is a long-time sojourner on our Island, and he considered "The Beast in the Jungle" perhaps James's greatest tale, that of a man "haunted only by his own fears. A story of mood and atmosphere and melancholy. It places James among the moderns, those who have sought to record the existential life of man."

Somerset Maugham did not agree. When he spent one of his wartime summers at Edgartown he was compiling an anthology of English literature to be sold in chain stores and drugstores at a low price to attract everyday kinds of people to writers they ought to know. He included "The Beast in the Jungle" but warned his readers that they might find it "exquisitely tedious." Maugham himself thought the story "a bitter revelation of the inadequacy James felt in himself. I will not spoil it by telling the secret that James through all these laborious pages has tantalizingly held out to the end, but that shortcoming that made a futility of his hero's life is, I fancy, the shortcoming that Henry James was too perspicacious not to recognize in himself . . . I do not quite believe in it as a narrative."

I think the story seemed hard going when I first read it

years ago. I had not then experienced the reward of coming upon such sentences as these: "The fate he had been marked for he had met with a vengeance — he had emptied the cup to the lees; he had been the one man of his time, *the* man to whom nothing on earth was to have happened." "The beast had lurked indeed, and the beast at its hour had sprung; it had sprung in the twilight of the cold April dawn when, pale, ill, wasted, but all beautiful, she had risen from her chair before him and let him imaginably guess."

Differences of opinion are among man's handsomest freedoms, and sometimes they surprise you. The other day I was reading Brendan Gill's theatrical criticism in *The New Yorker*, during the course of which he declared: "The arts are not a kindergarten. In them is no A for effort, only for excellence." Gill is happy in being able to recognize excellence when he sees it, though my training has made me sceptical of absolutes, and I recalled Gill's praise of *By Love Possessed* and how he had been left stranded when the tide went out.

Joseph Wood Krutch, whom I always admired, once wrote that novels exist "in order that critics may lay bare their symbolic or mythological content (often unsuspected by the novelist himself). Thus Mark Twain certainly did not know that *Huckleberry Finn* was, as one of the best-known contemporary critics has recently demonstrated — to his own satisfaction — a homosexual novel."

Much the same point is made by Ellen Glasgow in one of her prefaces collected in the volume, *A Certain Measure*: "Surely there can be no worse fashion in criticism than the practise of rebuking an author because he has not written another, and an entirely different, book, which he had no intention of writing, upon a subject of which he remains, whether happily or unhappily, ignorant. Just here one cannot do better than answer in Virginia Woolf's pointed words: 'Our gratitude largely takes the form of thanking them for having shown us what we certainly could not do, but as certainly do not wish to do.' "

Jane Austen protested disparagement of her craft: " 'Oh! It is only a novel!' replies the young lady while she lays down her book with affected indifference, a momentary shrug. It is only Cecelia, or Camilla, or Belinda, or, in short, some work in which the greatest powers of the mind are displayed, in which the most thorough knowledge of human nature, the happiest delineation of its varieties, the liveliest effusions of wit and humour, are conveyed to the world in the best-chosen language . . ."

If one is raising hell with the critics, he should not overlook Marcel Proust: ". . . I realized that I would have allowed her to belittle Maeterlinck (whom for that matter she now admired, from a feminine weakness of intellect, influenced by those literary fashions whose rays spread slowly), as I realized that Maeterlinck had belittled Baudelaire, Stendhal, Balzac, Paul-Louis Courier, Victor Hugo, Meilhac, Mallarmé. I realized that the critic had a far more restricted outlook than his victim, but also a purer vocabulary."

Pursuing the matter one step further, one may cite Sainte-Beuve (1804–1869) as he is found in *The Practical Cogitator*: "Nothing is more painful to me than the disdain with which people treat second-rate authors, as if there were room only for the first-raters."

The trouble is in identifying the second-raters within a contemporary range of vision. At any rate, there certainly is an A for effort in the arts, and probably a B and a C, Brendan Gill notwithstanding.

Survival values are a different matter. Irwin Edman, naturalistic philosopher, put this clearly in his essay, "Not for an Age." "Could anyone be better equipped than we are to free ourselves from the conventions which bound the earlier generations? Have we not seen around Marx and around liberalism and around Newton, even?"

And then: "Suddenly one hears the voice of posterity: 'How alike they all sound, the whole kit and caboodle of them, in the 1950s with their culture patterns, their freight of the new atomic age . . .' The voice sinks to a faint whisper: 'There were one or two original minds, but nobody paid any attention to them.' The voice trailed off almost into silence. For the life of me I could not make out what the names were. The voice repeated them, but since I had never heard of them before they meant nothing to me, and I forgot them at once."

One certainty is that some of us are flying high, so high that there seems no need for an earth under our feet.

David Lowenthal, a research geographer, wrote in the former *Columbia University Forum* to castigate most of us, especially the environmentalists, for an "animistic bias." He conceded that real disasters might come from tampering with nature, even as great as the destruction of mankind, but still worse was to stand in the way of man's "growing mastery over the environment."

The animists, he said, seek to influence and conciliate the "shifting and shadowy company of unknown powers or influences which reside in the primeval forest, in the crumbling hills, in the rushing river, in the spreading tree" — and so on. That is baldly and poetically stated, and I think it's nonsense. Mr. Lowenthal was in favor of civilization, and of man's conquest of the environment as an act of free will or of self-indulgence. He didn't say what man, but obviously it would be, and largely has been, economic man, assuring that the resources of the natural world must be exploited for profit. Anything less than calculated plunder of nature would be surrender to animistic bias.

Man, wrote Mr. Lowenthal, need not maintain any particular balance of nature in order to survive. He declared that "there is no inherent merit in a tree, a blade of grass, a flowing stream, or a good soil profile; if in a million years our descendants inhabit a planet of rock, air, ocean, and space ships, it would still be a world of nature." He wouldn't like it himself, but that is where his world would be headed. He is one who ought to pay special attention to the year 2000.

I still believe that animism, better termed naturalism, and a considerable persistence of mystery will continue on this planet that man did not make, in which his tenancy is by no means absolute, if, in John W. Gardner's words, we restrain "our Faustian zest in plunging after every technological possibility that promises profit or power or pleasure." If, as he adds, we cease to "act at once and live with the consequences." What chance remains that the condition, the all-important "if," will be fulfilled, is another matter.

A library, a fortress of a kind, with barriers no less real because they are intangible, is a secure place for thought. Even afternoon thoughts like mine are safe from assault. I looked around at the books on their shelves, and the other readers and searchers, old and young, and at the librarians at their desks or working at the card indexes. Here and for a few interludes of freedom, I could think contentedly, "So far, so good." No matter where we are going, here we are today.

As I left the library I smiled a grateful good-by to the women in charge, most of them known to me as girls when they were in school, and some not even in high school. I liked to see them here among the books; they helped me know exactly where I was, and to feel at home, and I made up my mind that I would return more often.

Where was I bound now? Well, I suppose I was going to rejoin Graham and set off with him for another walk around Sheriff's Meadow Pond. This was a happy intention because it meant that I needed no destination at all, though I might be indulging an animistic bias.

◇

Some of one's past years are almost certain to be carried as a burden, and we skip over them in nostalgia for earlier years and sometimes for the earliest of all that can be remembered.

We spent our summers during my boyhood in our old house in the country. We used to get out of bed early on Sunday morning and drive behind a steady, comfortable farm horse to Cottage City. There we boarded the excursion steamer that paddled through Vineyard Sound to the western promontory of Martha's Vineyard, the famous clay cliffs of Gay Head.

The early morning feeling, part of the excitement, would prolong itself into all our future years. Dawn would be in the sky already, but the pine trees still wore a ghost-like sheen in which they had spent a starlit night, and it was not until we had reached the main road that we saw the red-gold curve of the sun itself above a rim of oak trees. The main road formed a white ribbon under the arching trees, for it was compacted of water-bound crushed stone named after Mr. McAdam, the Scottish engineer.

Our drive was nothing we could boast of as a journey. The distance came to only about nine miles, requiring almost an hour and a half to traverse, but it boasted of itself in the hearts of my brother and me. By the time we reached Cottage City our subliminal selves felt they had traveled into a far country.

Cottage City changed on Sunday from holiday gaiety and noise to Sabbath pause and calm. Cottagers sat on their verandas, waiting for the full sacred peace of the day to unfold as the track of the sun crept across the little parks and gardens. Here and there a young man in cap, blazer, and tight bicycle pants would be pursuing an errand of his own, or a family group would stroll toward the Beatrice House or Frasier House for breakfast.

There was a high fence across the head of the wharf to keep summer crowds from the docking area, but the gate was opened to let us through because we had tickets. No freight or trucks on Sunday, no yelling hotel porters or shoeshine men, just the clean, expectant throng of excursionists whose shoes had been properly shined at home during the week. Other boys were as clean and glowing as my brother, who was eleven, and myself, who was eight.

Our tickets were taken at the gangplank by the purser, to whom we all said good morning, and my brother and I raced up the staircase from the main saloon to the open decks above. There we stood at the railing in fresh air and sunlight, looking out at the steeples, cottage roofs, and carriages arriving at the wharf. Many of the excursionists came aboard with boxes of saltwater taffy or popcorn, for which Cottage City was famous, but we felt no envy since we knew we were saving our appetites for fish chowder and lobster in a restaurant atop the cliffs at Gay Head.

A long blast of the boat's whistle, breaking the stillness, proved how complete the stillness had been. You don't hear that same quality of whistle any more because diesels have replaced steam along the coast. An old-time sidewheeler had one voice; a ferry has another — harsh, insensitive, and grating. No expectancy in it, or mourning of farewell. In the old days the steamboat whistle would be sounded to welcome the New Year, and it was a gracious resonance to turn over in bed to.

On weekdays the band would have been playing, but the special Sunday calm was much preferred for the making of an occasion such as this. The great, straining hawsers were cast off, allowing the boat to pull away from the wharf, though it appeared that the wharf was pulling away from us. We leaned over the rail, watching the water seethe and turn in lilypad pools, yeasting and circling.

Our boat would be the old *Nantucket* that had gilt and bright paint on the vanes of her paddleboxes. She steamed briskly across the open end of blue Vineyard Haven harbor, and when she rounded West Chop into the broad reaches of Vineyard Sound, the breeze strengthened, but only enough to make us feel that we were at sea and speeding along like one of the New York yachts, though not heeling as they did.

A young man's straw hat with its red and blue band was caught by a whiff of wind and carried astern into the white wake of the steamer while gulls circled over it. Younger women sat near the railing, or well forward on the open deck, near the pilot house if they could. Some were members of "parties," some were with young men in those popular striped blazers, and some were alone but contented. Older women in white blouses with flappy sleeves too big at the elbows, their hats tied on with veils, were more likely to be sitting amidships. Some retreated to the cabin when the wind blew too strongly into their faces.

The walking beam kept its rhythm, and why it walked — as it certainly did — I was not informed. The channel lay nearer to the Elizabeth Islands — Naushon, Nashawena, Pasque, and Cuttyhunk — than to our own Island, on account of our rocky shore and the Middle Ground shoal. We heard a bearded man, pointing, say to his wife, "That's Hadley's Harbor over there." My brother and I nudged each other, almost doubled with amusement, because we knew it was not Hadley's Harbor at all — it was Tarpaulin Cove with the white lighthouse we could see from our house in the North Shore hills of the Vineyard.

We knew, moreover, that Captain Kidd was supposed to have buried treasure at Tarpaulin Cove, and that the next stretch of the Naushon shore was the Old French Watering Place, and after that came the Black Woods, venerable forest of beech trees growing close to the shore.

Everyone's excitement increased as we turned and began to approach Gay Head. The tall cliffs presented a series of changing profiles of outjutting clay, great rugged masses of pure white, one escarpment of boldest, bravest red that we tried almost successfully to make out as an Indian profile; and other colors shading and blended with the deep contrasting green of bayberry thickets that had rooted at different elevations.

When we climbed the cliffs my brother and I liked to

choose the steepest places. We would also look for the blackness of the lignite in the Devil's Den. Now and then, we knew, a stroke of lightning would kindle the lignite into a smolder that started rumors of a volcanic eruption. Even Daniel Webster had supposed the cliffs to be of volcanic origin, but we knew that the force of glacial ice combined with the raising and lowering of the earth long ago had produced this wonder of nature.

We were hungry but not a bit fatigued when our parents found seats for us all in the plain board pavilion for our feast of chowder and lobster. Our father joked with us, charging that it was only appetite that had brought us, and that we really didn't care a whit about the spectacle of the cliffs. I took this seriously and protested that it was neither one nor the other, but both. My brother looked at me tolerantly and went on eating his chowder.

We were tired when we went back down the cliffs to board the steamer again at its crazy little pier, but neither my brother nor I would own up. We sat lazily steeped in the recessional quality of the excursion and the day. The westering sun followed us down the Sound and around West Chop, and the schooners and barges rode idly at their anchorages as we crossed Vineyard Haven harbor, the inward-bound view so different, as if we had come from far seas instead of only Gay Head. At last we bore down on the Cottage City wharf and warped in alongside in a stir of fuming water.

Then came the drive up-Island, so much longer now, and with ourselves so quiet that we heard contentedly almost every hoofbeat of the plodding horse.

Home again, with an afterglow of the excursion and the strangeness of having been all day absent from familiar things. Our parents said they didn't see how we could possibly be hungry, but my brother and I ate greedily of the steaming huckleberry potpie brought by lamplight to the dining room table.

⌣

There used to be a place on one of the wood roads where a path seemed to have turned off; but it must have been a mystery path, for it disappeared in a thicket of wild rose and bayberry. Finally we asked Mayhew G. Norton about it when we went in the morning for our milk, because the road was on his land. He was a big, craggy, kindly man, and he said he would go with us sometime and show us where the path led. He said it led to the Land of Beulah.

It pleased him to puzzle my brother and me, but presently he explained that in the old days Sunday School picnics had been held in a glade in these woods, and the glade was so full of peace and quiet, and he guessed of holiness, that it had been called by this name.

My brother and I were little acquainted with the Old Testament and even less with *Pilgrim's Progress*, but the Land of Beulah took our fancy on its own account. We decided we would not wait for Mr. Norton, but at the first opportunity we would press on through the thickets and find it by our own enterprise and discovery.

The chance came a day or two later, soon after the sunlight had streamed through our house and my father had gone back to the city and my mother was busy with her housework, which she always did determinedly in a way of her own.

This time we did not stop when we came to the thickets but pretended that the path still led straight on, or as

nearly straight as country paths are supposed to be. We
were soon in oak woods, through which the travel was
easier, and my brother, proud of being a pathfinder, said
he could see traces of a once-trodden way. I was not so sure.

We had gone not quite half a mile, I would guess, when
the way led steeply downward, and the oak woods yielded
to beech and maple because, as we soon found, a brook
trickled through the hollow into which we descended, and
on either side the trees rooted in damp soil. A little beyond
the brook we saw the brightly sunlit glade we had been
told about. A drift of boulders, some large, some small and
flat enough to sit upon, lay across the open, mossy ground,
and most of these boulders bore lichens in designs that
might have been mystic ciphers if one called upon imagination with enough art.

Peace and quiet, the stillness emphasized by faint rustling of leaves, could never have been a greater delight. We
were under a spell. The warmth of the sun, the caress of
summer air, and the mixed coolness of dark beech trees
made us want to sit and wait and experience something to
come, we didn't know what.

My brother pointed, indicating that I should look at a
bird, mostly black and white, that was going nimbly up
and down the smooth gray bole of a giant beech. He knew
about birds already and began arguing with himself in a
whisper as to whether this was a downy woodpecker or a
black and white warbler. I was of no help. The only birds
I knew were robins, catbirds, chewinks, and whippoorwills, the last because they came at dusk to perch on our
stone doorstep and reiterate their strange, fascinating call.
No other birds could pronounce words as whippoorwills
did.

So it was I who glanced past the tree and the bird and

saw a boy and a girl across the glade. There had been no
sound of footsteps, but obviously these two had approached
from a direction opposite to ours.

The boy was a little taller and leaner than my brother,
with dark hair and smooth skin. I knew he was not an Indian, but he had the right darkness and lithe presence, and
should have been something more than a farm boy, even if
not quite an Indian. His sister, as she proved to be, must
have been about my age, and I thought her pretty, though
at that time I had few thoughts about girls other than that
they existed and demanded acknowledgement. Her eyes
were blue, her skin pink and white, and her hair the color
of corn silk close to the ear in early summer. This much I
could see as well as anyone, perhaps better, because I was
not biased by notions of romance.

The moment was one of adventure, and after a few moments of awkwardness at the beginning, we found ourselves grouped on the most convenient boulders, talking in
lively fashion. The boy was Whitten Spinney, called Whit,
and his sister was Thamosin, called Tammy. My brother
and I knew that the Spinney farm was vaguely removed
from our own part of the countryside, and that it had the
sanction of antiquity and a kind of thrift you took for
granted in New England, though our parents agreed it
was dying out.

Whit and Tammy knew about the Sunday School picnics, though not who had held them or how long ago, but
they did not know that this was the Land of Beulah, as we
had the delight of informing them.

What we talked about during that first time of meeting
and discovery is not my secret, for I lost track of it years
and years ago, and would pay a big price to relearn any
small part. But we spoke of the glade, its magic, and how

it would be our secret place and we would come here often.

My brother produced two bananas he had secreted in his overalls before we left the house, unknown to me. He should have told me and I would have done the same. I deplored my own lack of foresight, but I did have a few untidy peanuts in my pants pocket. We divided this provender, and Whit found some berries of the tall shrub the old people called wild pear, sugary and insipid, but good enough to help out the occasion. We drank out of the brook, lying flat.

We anointed ourselves mystically behind the ears with the red juice of pokeweed, or a plant that seemed like it, and buried a token under the tallest side of the biggest boulder, scooping out the damp earth with our hands. The token consisted of half a dozen shingle nails contributed by Whit. They were never to be dug up unless all four of us were there together.

When my brother and I reached home, my mother asked where we had been, and I waited anxiously to hear what my brother would say. He said, "Out in the woods." My mother didn't ask about the red stains behind our ears and running down our necks, because she naturally thought we had been playing Indians, and this shows how very long ago these happenings were.

Only we, and Whit and Tammy, nobody else, knew that we had been in the Land of Beulah and planned to go there on sunny days again and again.

$\diamond$

We had no horse of our own then. It was Mayhew G. Norton's horse, a sorrel named Connie, we hired by the day when we took long outings. Later on, I speculated on how

closely Connie might resemble Tom Faggus's strawberry
mare in *Lorna Doone*. I was not sure I could recognize a
strawberry mare.

It was another Sunday when we went on a journey of
discovery to Makoniky, six or seven miles away to the eastward of our house on the glacial ridge that ran more or
less parallel to Vineyard Sound, broken in many places by
swamps and ravines as it subsided to the shore. At Makoniky there was a brickworks at some distance from an
abandoned summer hotel that stood echoing and empty in
the ruin of its great expectations. Dirt roads led down to
the Sound, and a ramshackle pier served for the loading of
bricks on schooners for shipment to the mainland.

The kiln, big-bellied, seemed to be partly dismantled,
but this was because it was awaiting newly moulded bricks
to be built into it for the firing. Railroad tracks, narrow-
gauge and not free of rust, supported two-wheel dump
trucks that brought clay from nearby pits and took finished
bricks to the shore and pier.

Not many bricks were being made, but an Armenian
potter, a gentle old man who spoke to us in a kindly way,
shaped pottery for glazing and baking, to fill in his time
and to make use of space in the kiln. There was no fire for
us to see now, but our imaginations could picture immense
heat, represented by the blackened remains of past firings.
The old potter showed us how he could "throw" pitchers,
vases, plates, and so on, using his wheel, and how he made
"slip" do the bidding of his supple hands.

After a while my brother and I went off by ourselves,
and by removing a few boards from a batten, obtained entrance to the old hotel. The summer air had been shut out,
so that at first we were shivery, and I thought my teeth

would chatter. But we warmed ourselves nicely by running back and forth along the corridors and up and down the stairs, finally peering into this room and that, most of them empty of furniture but a few with beds, bureaus, and chairs. We climbed all the way to the top, three stories up, and then to the cupola, which was higher still. We could see across Vineyard Sound, across Naushon and Buzzard's Bay, and to the mill chimneys and church towers of New Bedford in a blue, blue distance.

Then we went down to the hotel office, where my brother, as room clerk, checked me in as a guest. He inquired whether I had any baggage, and I was lost as to a proper answer.

"You should say you have two trunks that are checked through and will arrive on the stage on Tuesday," my brother told me, and added, "Stupid!"

This last was no more than an ordinary brotherly interjection that could be interpreted as encouragement. We went on playing hotel until finally we became tired of the game.

On the way home behind the plodding Connie, we congratulated ourselves on having found another extension of our summer excursions and adventures, a renewable experience within reach, an added dimension of a life that was and would be our own.

So I tell of what we remember of the things we used to do long ago when we were boys, and in that phrase "used to" I find an inexhaustible magic. It is a funny phrase, really, as familiar as any, and whoever thinks to look it up?

I looked it up just now: *Usage.* The following examples illustrate *use* as an auxiliary verb in positive, negative, and interrogatory constructions: *He used to go there. He used not to go* (or *did not use to go*). *Did* (or *didn't*) *he used to go?"* These are from the *American Heritage Dictionary.*

Every time we say we used to do something long ago, memory rises up a little, or turns over, or glistens in a sunlight that may not have been above the horizon for fifty years or more.

These are the things we used to do, yet not one of the experiences I have described was ever repeated in the life of my brother or myself. None of them, nor any of a dozen others, was done more than once. It is a mirage of recollection and nostalgia that supplies the wonderful claim of repetition.

We took the excursion steamer to Gay Head on one Sunday and never again; we intended to go back to the Land of Beulah but time, interrupting, passed on — and all at once we were older; Makoniky in the state we knew it vanished after that single season. They remain in their exclusiveness, the experiences that were ours and can never be for anyone in the world again.

〜

There are also the middle years of memory, and I shy away from them more often than not. Nostalgia in that retrospect is quite different and often bitter. We long ago stopped being the children we once were and can look back upon them, not as ourselves, but as characters in a finished play. We may claim or disclaim them as we like in their closed chapter of the past and may even be fond of them without feeling any responsibility. But in the middle years we face ourselves not only as we were, but a good deal as we are now.

I don't think I like "middle" as a modifier. I prefer

"age" alone. Middle age makes the mistake of never having outlived its youth, or of not knowing whether it has or not. To cling to youth can be satisfying only up to a certain point, and one should decide wisely when to let go. Middle age should not be allowed to drag, either, and a consolation may be that to free oneself from that period of life and to become at last somewhat fond of it, one must be securely old.

In some novel lately I read, "Whom the gods hate, they keep forever young." But the gods have no choice, for all of us do get rid of youth at last, no matter how tardily. Some prefer a cynical point of view, as in Proust: "This perpetual error which is, precisely, life . . ." So if we like we can say that, young or old, it makes no difference.

I have been looking into middle years I know are finished, but without real willingness to accept the finality. The past is not recent, but recent enough so that I can pretend it is still going on, or at least not yet out of reach.

I have found old letters written by Betty during her life on the *Gazette* when she was editing the rural correspondence, among so many other things, thirty years ago.

"I think I should try to make clear to you," she wrote to one correspondent, "that we are depending on you to vary the monotony of your items. I was ill last week and unable to copy-read your notes as I usually do. As a result, practically every item contains the word 'returned.'

"Now there are many ways in which one can say that a person has returned. He can 'come home,' 'get back,' 'reach home,' or just 'be home' from a trip. Furthermore, both last week and particularly this week you have used 'recently' in a large proportion of your items. 'Recently' is not good enough. If people were away this week we should say so, or at the Christmas period, or over the holidays, but a continuous succession of 'recentlys' leads everyone to believe that this is very old stuff, in addition to tiring them with the repetition. I think it is only fair that the correspondents should attempt to make their copy as interesting and unhackneyed as possible."

This reminded me of a wry complaint by a much earlier writing woman, Jane Austen, in *Northanger Abbey*: ". . . and this is a very nice day; and we are taking a very nice walk; and you are two very nice young ladies. Oh! It's a very nice word indeed! It does for everything . . ."

The *Gazette*'s competition in the days I now recall was a mainland daily that printed a Cape and Island edition. Some of our correspondents helped themselves from the columns of our rival, and Betty's vigilance was always catching them at it.

> Dear Mrs. Riley,
>
> I should like to call your attention to an error in your copy which could only have come from the *Standard-Times* items.
>
> You referred to a guest of Mrs. Charles G. Norton as Philip Ordway. The guest was, in fact, Priscilla Ordway. Once more I implore you not to take *Standard-Times* items, especially without checking them, and I also implore you to get your copy in early while we are in such a frightful rush here.

But we were always in a rush, or so it seemed. We got tired and were in need of a good deal of pumping up and recruiting of our spirits to go on as we ought. Betty wrote:

> Dear Lois,
>
> Of the 17 items on your sheet this week, 14 were about guests, and 12 of them said: "is — or are — the guest or guests of so-and-so for the week." Will you please vary the monotony and save me the extra trouble?

Betty and I both kept journals from time to time, off and on, but mostly off as our good intentions failed and as other chores eroded our energies. I thought I would copy out some of Betty's good-day entries and some of her bad-day entries, but all days were the same, a mixture of good and bad. This is the bitterness and the sweetness of the middle years when at last they have marched away with so little achievement and satisfaction.

Thursday, the day before publication of the *Gazette*, stood for ordeal and challenge. One Thursday in February Betty wrote:

Nasty day except for a few interludes. Very strong wind for a few hours around noon. Medium-cold with tiny bits of snow in A.M. Quite a busy day. Florence out with cold, but Olga came in cheerily in the afternoon and we all left about 5:45. West Tisbury and Chilmark town meetings and news about the new chairman of the Steamship Authority, who seems a good choice. We even praised Governor Herter for naming him. Emily H. brought in her two poodle puppies for me to see. Moonlight tonight for the first time in days. Not much bird news.

Not all bad, not all good; some weariness and too little fun in looking ahead:

A rough day for all of us, I guess. Very fine and bright outdoors but cool. Snowed under with work. Copy heavy, mostly with Scout and 4-H news, but lots of court to write up. Worried about how we'll pull through with the big Invitation Edition. *So much to do.* Nothing really exciting to report on a day like this.

Now a Thursday with a difference. The McCarthy mystique was over the Island as over the country:

A pretty good April 1. I fooled Everett and he fooled me, according to established practice. The weather fooled us all, starting out quite beautifully, then getting bad, with faint snow flurries. Greatly upset by one awful McCarthy letter from George Ellis, who only last September called the *Gazette* the best small paper in America. Everett said he was glad there was one person who agreed with him. It is ignorance and the terrible influence of the *Standard-Times*, which is all for McCarthy.

Everett was our Number Two man in the back shop, and since we had only two, he was important. George Ellis had begun his letter to the *Gazette*, "A light has gone out." We had taken an unequivocal editorial stand against the in-flammatory campaign of Senator McCarthy, treating the issue not only as national but local, and it was not at all certain how we would come out. We allied ourselves with Gerald Chittenden, retired master of St. Paul's School, who had set up an anti-McCarthy table in his Borrowdale Book-shop at Edgartown. He chose to call himself a noncompeti-tive man and wrote a book about being a resident expatri-ate, and he was both an old-school Republican and conservative, but he was no looker-on. Books on his anti-McCarthy table included Elmer Davis's *But We Were Born Free*, Orwell's *1984* and *Animal Farm*, Aldous Hux-ley's *Brave New World*, and so on, not overlooking the writings of Tom Paine.

Most of those who wrote to the *Gazette* were against us, but we heard from some supporters. Betty wrote:

Got to the office early. The boys printed the first section of the Invitation Edition. O.K., but somehow not a master-piece, 6500 pressrun. Heard a purple finch sing this A.M. Reverend W. M. Thompson came out in church leaflet vs. McCarthy, which I hope had some effect on the girls. Ham again with sweet potatoes and marshmallow. Music, sleep-ing, and reading. Joe Sylvia has gone to town in a big way to save the beach.

"Wintry and more so as the day progresses. A not very productive morning," Betty wrote. "Reading V. Woolf tonight and nearing end. Mrs. Edey and Earl Haynes support us against McCarthy. Whitethroats came early . . ." Later: "Louis Graves has sold the *Chapel Hill Weekly* and I am bereft. He'll keep on contributing." "Old grind as to weekend, and too much mess all over the place, Augean stable–style, but I struggled along somehow." "The demolition of the icehouse is proceeding, with the roof nearest us bare and open to the sky already."

A note of my own: "Saw Theodore Wimpenney and remarked on his status as the oldest male citizen. When I went across the street to speak to him, Mr. Annas, the Methodist minister, went with me and congratulated Theodore on his state of preservation and so on, expressing a wish that he live ten years more. 'Well,' Theodore said, 'I'm in no hurry to go.' "

It was this way with us on D-day in World War II:

Woke up about 6. Sunny morning and warmer. Up at 6:30 and a minute before 7 turned on the radio and heard Kaltenborn's name mentioned — the invasion was on. Hurried upstairs to tell Betty and she said she knew when she heard me coming. She said, "I say the bells should ring." So I called Mr. Thompson and then Mr. Annas, neither of whom had heard the news. But the St. Andrew's bells began first, and then the Congo, and last the Methodist. Called Bill, tried to get the Dillons, and Betty finally got Curtis Moffat, who had had a premonition last night. A fine June day, clear, blue-skied and sunny. *Rosa rugosa* coming out and fragrant. Our routine about as usual, but Betty stopped in St. Andrew's at noon and again after supper. And we listened until 8 A.M., again at noon, and again after supper to the radio. A solemn but quiet atmosphere in town. All flags out, everywhere. School committee meeting this afternoon.

We had known about the outgrowing of childhood and youth, but we had not thought much, if at all, about what came next and how temporary we and our concerns would turn out to have been. How odd now to think of concern about news of Scouts and 4-H Clubs. We had little warning of the Age of Strangers, little real misgiving about the future of a town that had aged so well through generations and centuries.

It happens to be a sunny April morning as I am typing these lines, and with no effort at all I can see Betty at her typewriter over by the window, the sunlight streaming in upon her white hair that once was twinkling brown, a blue sweater around her shoulders. Her tongue is pressed lightly against the inside of one cheek, and her blue eyes look intently at the sheet in her typewriter. The books and papers on her desk are rounded up like a bulwark, and at last she smiles.

No one but myself would be aware that she has been giving some advertiser or correspondent living hell, but in the end neither one would mind.

Everything about our life, Graham's and mine, all our walks, explorations, encounters, and adventures, in sunny days of spring or autumn, or the bitter days and nights of winter, the changing look of Sheriff's Meadow Pond, have a secret spell of sentiment and memory. Graham's span is shorter than mine, but he likes to go where he has been before. It is the same with him as it is with me.

But in the modern world sentiment is not intellectually respectable unless it is disguised, as, for instance, in Disney's *Snow White* or the illusory heroines of Hemingway or some favorite cartoon strip. I am aware, though, of voices on the other side. Charles P. Curtis, educated at Groton, Harvard, and the Ecole des Sciences Politiques in

Paris, member of the Harvard faculty, a classicist, and a big-game hunter into the bargain — however that may be said to fit in — wrote in his *A Commonplace Book*: ". . . a good man is something less than a whole man if he is not sentimental. Angels can weep but not laugh. Men can do both. Tom Jones bursts into tears repeatedly. The toughest hero of them all, Odysseus, weeps. The tears ran down his cheeks when he heard Demodocus, the minstrel, sing of Troy, and he pulled his mantle across his face, and when Demodocus sang again, Odysseus again wept . . . Odysseus was sitting with the tears running down his face on the headland of Calypso's island, looking toward Ithaca, "when Hermes brought word that Odysseus was to go home."

No matter what professions they may make about sentiment, all writers tend to look far off at Ithaca, or at some spring or summer in France, with the tenderest feeling. It occurs to me to cite passages from two novels of quite different character. The first:

> There were whole streets — and these by no means the least fascinating and romantic — where the unwritten domestic records of every house were afloat in the air outside it — records not all savory and sweet, but always full of interest and charm.
>
> One knew at a sniff as one passed the porte cochère what kind of people lived behind and above; what they ate and drank; and what their trade was; whether they did washing at home, and burned tallow or wax, and mixed chicory with their coffee, and were overfond of Gruyère cheese — the biggest, cheapest, plainest and most formidable cheese in the world; whether they fried with oil or butter, and liked their meats overdone and garlic in their salad . . .
>
> And here, as I write, a mere nostalgic fancy, compound,

generic, synthetic and all-embracing — an abstract olfactory symbol of the "Tout Paris" of fifty years ago — comes back to me out of the past; and fain would I inhale it in all its pristine freshness and vigor. For scents, like musical sounds, are rare sublimates of the essence of memory . . . Oh, that I could hum or whistle an old French smell! I could evoke all Paris, sweet pre-Imperial Paris, in a single whiff.

The second:

. . . the carriage suddenly seemed to run more easily, more softly and noiselessly; the streets through which I was passing were those of long-forgotten paths . . . The soil knew of itself where it was to go; its resistance was overcome. And like an aviator who has been laboriously rolling along the ground and then suddenly takes off, I rose slowly toward the silent heights of memories past. In all Paris those streets will always stand out for me as of a different substance from the others. When I reached the corner of the Rue Royale . . . it seemed to me as if the carriage, guided by my habit of turning that corner so many times, could not possibly do otherwise than turn of its own accord. I was not passing through the same streets as the strollers who were abroad that day, but through a past that glided softly, sad and sweet.

Both writers, one remembered now by only a few, the other secure as one of the greatest of the world's novelists, were looking back, looking toward Ithaca, evoking that kind of nostalgia familiar to us all as one of the deepest of sentiments. The first passage is from George Du Maurier's *Peter Ibbetson*, the second from Marcel Proust's *Remembrance of Things Past*.

At the risk of overdoing comparisons, I hope I may offer two more:

A little girl, with fair, reddish hair, who appeared to be returning from a walk, and held a trowel in her hand, was looking at us, raising toward us a face powdered with pinkish freckles. Her black eyes gleamed, and . . . since I had not, as they say, enough "power of observation" to isolate the sense of their colour, for a long time afterwards whenever I thought of her, the memory of those bright eyes would at once present to me as a vivid azure, since her complexion was fair . . . she allowed her eyes to wander, over the space that lay between us, in my direction, without any particular expression, without appearing to have seen me, but with an intensity, a half-hidden smile which I was unable to interpret, according to the instruction I had received in the ways of good breeding, save as a mark of infinite disgust; and her hand, at the same time, sketched in the air an indelicate gesture for which, when it was addressed in public to a person whom one did not know, the little dictionary which I carried in my mind supplied only one meaning, namely a deliberate insult.

Fourth and last:

Her poor little daughter, the object of her passionate solicitude, a very clever and precocious child, was the reverse of beautiful, although she would have had fine eyes but for her red lashless lids. She wore her thick hair cropped short, like a boy, and was pasty and sallow in complexion, hollow-cheeked, thick-featured and overgrown, with long, thin hands, and arms and legs of quite pathetic length and tenuity, a silent and melancholy little girl, who sucked her thumb perpetually and kept her own counsel. She would have to lie in bed for days together, and when she got well enough to sit up I (to please her mother) would read *Les Robinsons Suisses* . . . *Les Contes* of Charles Perrault, the shipwreck of Don Juan, of which we never tired . . .

The first little girl, with reddish hair, pink freckles, and the vulgar gesture, became Marcel Proust's fair-complexioned Mademoiselle De Forcheville, whom, when he met her under that name, he had already loved and now thought only of possessing, the same but so different Gilberte Swann, remembered from his boyhood. And the little girl with red lashless lids, "poor little Mimsi, toujours mal à la tête," became Du Maurier's loveliest of women, the Duchess of Towers.

To suggest that for the purpose of introducing the early and unpromising phase of a predestined beauty the two passages might be interchanged, is allowable, though readers must decide for themselves how far either passage could be extended without giving the show away. The genuineness of sentiment is obvious — a bit more in one case than the other? I would not know which, and anyway what of that?

The vogue of shunning sentiment or sentimentality, when the distinction is blurred as it so often is, may be exposed as one of the great impersonations, on the level of Hemingway and the artificial hair on his chest. Your critic of the sentimental in literature is likely to be some neurotic professor in middle life whose subconscious urge is to get back inside his mother's womb. Though subconscious, the notion is still preposterous, and who is he, with his subliminal longing, to lecture the rest of us?

I see no shame in the shared quality of feeling, no matter how tenderly or sensitively held, though perspective and proportion do have their importance. At times we weep with Odysseus or shed tears out of longing for Ithaca, and it is natural that we should. Our tears may be for lost love and youth, or any of the lost things Thomas Wolfe wrote about. The lostness is what counts.

The sentiment in *Remembrance of Things Past* is mixed

with other realities, but it is strongly and recurringly present. Mixed with cynicism, yes: The characterization of "a man with a receding brow and eyes that dodge between the blinkers of his education and his prejudices" catches us all at least a bit; this is the dodging we all do. And there is the admonition that we live "in a world of very nearlies, where people salute the empty air and arrive at wrong judgments." The health of democracy hangs not so much by a thread as on a blinking.

But cynicism disappears when Proust is sentimental. "To be with people one loves, to speak to them or not to speak to them, it is all the same." "When the mind has a tendency to dream, it is a mistake to keep dreams away from it, to ration its dreams . . ." "Existence to us is hardly interesting save on the days on which the dust of realities is shot with the magic sand, on which some trivial incident of life becomes a spring of romance . . ."

When Betty and I had been thirty years with the *Vineyard Gazette*, which then seemed a long time, an old sentiment rose warmly with spring freshness in us both. I looked back and wrote of the time of our beginning, and how the time had been then:

> Thirty years ago the post office opened at 7 in the morning and closed following the arrival of mail on the late boat. There is no late boat any more, many of the citizens who stirred early are dead, and the post office keeps more orthodox hours; you can no longer follow the sunlight up the street and see Herbert Breen in his long duster sweeping the sidewalk and getting in the first day's gossip with Abel Doane from the dry-goods store. But if there are ghosts from the town's past they will find their way here, early and late. They will read our mail over our shoulders and listen avidly to the news we exchange.

At any time of day the town is still beautiful; even in negligent and ordinary details it is beautiful, for these cannot disparage the white houses, the trees, the old easy but uncompromising sense of order, the pattern set about us. We like the streets piled with snow in winter or drifted with autumn leaves or lined with rambler roses and large-flowered climbers in June. The town takes well to all seasons, and there is always the moving harbor, its color, its restlessness. There is always the dome of sky looking down upon a small place, and upon men, women, children, and animals who follow the seasons and the years through lives that in spite of frictions and difficulties are merged into one life, that of the town itself.

I wrote this thirty years ago, and suppose it must have been true, and I wonder at what period in the succeeding years it stopped being true. I know now that although I like to think and write of ghosts from the town's past, there are no such ghosts unless, for a little while, I am one myself. I know that the town has lost its contentment. Most of its active and important people have resumed in new and harsh ways the old quest of wealth and power, though I knew an interlude of faith, purpose, and respite that I believe would have endured longer but for the destruction of values in World War I. Nothing now can withstand the erosion of time, custom, television, migration, and new enterprise in these changeling decades during which the unhappy imperatives are growth and change.

I met Eli Ginzberg at Chappaquansett the other day. We were at a cocktail party and I saw him coming toward me, and he asked, "Has the decline of the Vineyard been more or less rapid than you expected?"

"Much more rapid," I said.

"It's been much less rapid than I expected," he said.

"That's the difference between an economist and an environmentalist."

I thought that over for a while, and later I said to myself, "Anyway, we had the best of it."

WE WERE AT THE DUNES restaurant for dinner last night, and it turned out that a double birthday was being celebrated at a table not quite out of earshot, part way across the room. The senior member of the celebration was, I suppose, about my age, and the junior member had reached the age of seven. There were eight or ten in the birthday group, mostly family, apparently, and some friends who had almost family status. The Happy Birthday song was sung, the lighted cake brought in, the candles blown out, and happiness prevailed so easily that I am sure not one of the party felt how this birthday like all others was ebbing slowly but irrevocably away.

Oddly, perhaps, I found myself identifying not so much

with the old gentleman who was my contemporary, but with the child of seven. I recall few birthdays as separate and distinct — the most recent one, of course — and most clearly, or perhaps most sentimentally, the occasion of November 8, 1903.

My mother read to me Jean Ingelow's poem, "Seven Times One Is Seven" which begins, irrelevantly I thought then, "There's no dew left on the daisies and clover / There's no rain left in heaven." How puzzled I was then, and how fondly I now look back upon that poem, the kind of fondness that is not far removed from a certain wistfulness and longing.

> I am old, so old I can write a letter;
> My birthday lessons are done;
> The lambs play always, they know no better;
> They are only one times one.

As to that most recent November day when I became eighty-two, I am, of course, quite aware of most of the events — not too many to have kept track of — and not only my thoughts at the time but with later embellishments added. Most other birthdays, running back through the years, make me think of Stephen Vincent Benét's image of summers gone "like faded marigolds in the long-gathered hay."

I find that tiresome sop to the aging, "A man is as old as he feels," not so cheap as I used to consider it. A dear friend and distinguished physician, Dr. Leona Baumgartner, has assured me that chronological age is not *that* important. Leona is right, of course. All the same, and this occurred to me again last night, I have private information that I am growing older not only by a count of birthdays but by the passage of time in between.

Friends and acquaintances say to me, "How well you look," and some one of the acquaintances, possibly just arrived from the city for his vacation, is likely to spoil it all by remarking, "You look so much better than when I saw you last year." The thought of what this person may say to me a year from now is downright chilling.

How I feel on any birthday is due more to circumstance than to age. When I am asked whether I feel older than I did yesterday I will always say that I do not, and this is likely to be fractionally true. The word "old" does not define any feeling properly related to one's time of life. A spell of arthritis may be due to weather or lack of sleep. When a youth gets up in the morning suffering from acne and unrequited love, he does not say he is feeling *young*. The child at the party last night showed all the signs of being happily young, but I am pretty sure she felt happily old.

On the credit side of aging is the principle of recurrence. In her volume of poems, *What's O'Clock*, Amy Lowell says: "Days and days — what then? / Is not recurrence a smile on the face of age?" I have been here before, one says to oneself, and what does it matter that the hour is later now? To have lived another year by the calendar is something, and to have lived alertly through the march of seasons completes the measure, until as time passes one values more and more the privilege of looking back. Reflections and memories take on a cherished patina as they are added to the possessions of later life.

One of the things I have most securely learned is that I must not believe anything without doubt. Live with this principle long enough and you acquire a clearer outlook. I think of the admonition of Oliver Cromwell: "My brethren, by the bowels of Christ I beseech you, bethink that you may be mistaken." Cromwell is not well remembered for an open mind, and that is part of the lesson, too.

I am as much aware of the need to have convictions, and though they may be held off for a reasonable length of time as hypotheses, in the end they amount to belief and must be stuck to. This is difficult ground on which to stand, doubt on one side and convictions on the other, and always with a hope of learning more. One certainty I do accept, and this is the existence of the unknowable. Since this certainty may be taken as a variant of doubt, there is no real contradiction.

One Sunday when Thoreau was twenty-two and on a country walk around Concord, he decided that he preferred Pan for a god, Pan "who still reigns in his pristine glory, with his ruddy face, his flowing beard, and shaggy body, his pipe and his crook, his nymphs and his chosen daughter, Iambe . . ."

He went on: "It seems to me that the god commonly worshiped in civilized countries is not at all divine, though he bears a divine name, but he is the overwhelming authority and respectability of mankind combined."

This bears comparison with the concept of Irwin Edman: "From partial cases of good and happiness men imagine a heaven which is compacted of these. The theologian tells us with elaborate demonstration of dogmatic faith that such a world does exist. The naturalist tells us that it does not, and that when with adult eyes we become accustomed to daylight we shall not miss the night of myth, the Heaven that appeared as a dream, and the gods created by desire."

A cautionary example of creation by desire is surely Ralph Waldo Emerson's dictum: "The blazing evidence of immortality is our dissatisfaction with any other solution."

Sometimes when I wake in the morning earlier than usual, often on days of early sunrise, I review some imagined fundamentals. Recently I found myself reflecting upon one of the funniest of short stories, "Inflexible Logic," by Russell Maloney, based upon what he termed "an old cliché of the mathematicians," that six chimpanzees, "just pounding away at the typewriter keys, would be found to copy out all the books ever written by man. There are only so many combinations of letters and numerals, and they'd produce all of them . . ."

It occurred to me, lying in bed, that given all eternity for the working of mathematical laws and the bringing together of all the possible combinations of matter-energy, the substances of my body might come together again in a distant future as the habitation of another creature. Allowance must be made for entropy, but perhaps not much. I wondered what the reconstituted creature might be like, and if he might live among the stars. My own mortality would not be extended, but I found agreeable the thought that clay of mine might join, unremembering, in adventures of far-off time. As a concern of mine, the year 2000 might not amount to much, after all.

But more likely, I think, the planet Earth will be destroyed by nuclear fire, and I hope there may be a special black hole in the sky for intelligences that destroy themselves.

Lately I have been collecting quotations in a more modest range, all having to do with age, such as these:

Santayana in *The Last Puritan*: "He was young but had put on age in his youth." Not the real thing, though, and he could not be entitled to membership in the Association of Retired Persons. George Eliot in *Daniel Deronda*: "A man's happiness is apt to show signs of wear until restored by second childhood." I must wait to see how it goes. William Jovanovich in an essay in *The American Scholar*: "Every man is a traveler from another time, and if the journey is long he ends as a stranger."

E. M. Forster in *A Passage to India*: "The twilight of double vision in which many elderly people are involved." To command some of past and some of present is not a bad thing, especially from a high point of vantage. James Russell Lowell: "In the parliament of the present every man represents a constituency of the past."

Shirley Hazzard in her novel, *Bay of Noon*: "Chronological age is tenacious, once attained it can't be shed; it increases, moment by moment, day by day, pressing its honours on you until you are over-endowed with them." I think of this when some pretty girl offers to carry my bundles for me. But my notion is that the word "honours" has been replaced by "status" and that too few of us know the difference.

I remember when Julia Earl and Alice Barker started a restaurant upstairs where the *Gazette* office used to be. We were at lunch there one day when Chester Ashley Pease happened to be sitting at a table nearby. He was known around town as Foolish Chester, not in any unkind spirit, to distinguish him from the other Chester. Out of a hum of usualness he spoke up, addressing us all: "Guess who's the oldest person in this room." Knives and forks remained poised. Silence continued for a moment while Chester looked around, smiling.

"I am," he said, relishing a moment entirely his own.

Sometimes in some establishment far more elaborate and pretentious than that of Julia Earl and Alice Barker so long ago, I am tempted to emulate Chester, and, perhaps tapping on my water glass first with a spoon to attract attention, put the same challenge: "Guess who's the oldest person in this room." Of course I don't do this, and although I have the answer ready, I keep it to myself.

Some aging people say they need more sleep now than when they were younger, but the opposite is more often true. I need less sleep now, but that little comes to me grudgingly. Nights are usually an ordeal to be gotten through as by heroic endurance.

On the morning of my eighty-second birthday Graham and I were up well before five and, breakfast over, embarked on our walk to the Harbor Light. The morning was on the gray side, and Starbuck's Neck brooded with a chill in the air. The light flashed dutifully and monotonously, without special effect. The Chappaquiddick ferry, making an early passage from the Point, did for a moment evoke a fantasy of voyaging, but not enough to change the direction of my thoughts.

As Graham and I walked home through Cottage Street the pretty girl we used to meet walking her yellow Lab puppy came out into her yard, almost to the fence, and said, "Happy birthday, Mr. Hough." Call this a little thing, but I'll remember it.

Not so long ago I was interviewed for a program on public radio, and now I listened to the tape sent to me by the thoughtful producer, Deborah Amos. I was surprised to hear myself saying in a foggy voice that I had never gotten over the habit of feeling young. This sounded brazenly sententious, a cliché at that, and I would have disowned it if I could, but Noah Adams, the interviewer, had carried us along so easily that my "habit of feeling young" slipped out easily from my background of having grown up a younger brother and one of the youngest kids on our block.

I am asked if I do not consider myself lucky, and of course I do, because survival in a state of good health is also good luck, and no mistake. Having had the right ancestors is a particularly good piece of luck. To avoid a charge of hubris, I think I should set down a number of entries on the deficit side. I don't think anyone comes out entirely in the clear.

A candidate for public office, even a president in the White House, nowadays reports what he has in the bank, what he owes, and to whom. As an octogenarian who also wants to keep the record straight, I will set off against an ostentation of good health some past and present liabilities: three hernia operations, all three on the right side; a prostatectomy; surgery for a tunnel syndrome in my right wrist, this last as an outpatient in and out of Massachusetts General Hospital, in preparation for which I stayed overnight at the Ritz, the first such indulgence in my career. I have some arthritis, diverticulitis that requires that I stow away as much bran every day as a horse, and I have trouble getting shoes that fit.

A while ago I said to Dr. Bob Nevin, "I can't hear as well as I used to." He said, "Neither can I."

I made a sea voyage to Woods Hole and by car to West Falmouth, where I saw a specialist. He showed me my chart, with lines going down hill from what I could hear to what I couldn't.

"You are getting to be what is called hard of hearing," he said, "and there's not a blessed thing that can be done about it." If some frequencies should be amplified, this would raise the devil with others, and I wouldn't be able to endure the distortion. Just the same, I would like to try an old-fashioned ear trumpet. The specialist told me to come back next year, and I liked the sound of this. Anyone who talks about next year in this way is an optimist.

The worst part of being hard of hearing, I find, is that many times you miss only one word, and when you ask what it was, you have the whole sentence boomed at you. For instance, you hear, ". . . said she would be here for the weekend and would make a point of looking you up at the *Gazette* office." You naturally want to know who "she" is, and when you ask this one thing, as modestly as possible, you get the full treatment: "EMILY SAID SHE WOULD BE HERE FOR THE WEEKEND AND WOULD MAKE A POINT OF LOOKING YOU UP AT THE *GA-ZETTE* OFFICE." This is a tremendous waste of fire power and belittling to the ego of the recipient.

So now I have told all, and feel as free as a cabinet minister who has made a clean breast of his affairs and in spite of some shady items is not to be indicted. When anyone asks me how I feel, I say, "Fine!", without intending any deceit, because I do feel fine most of the time.

～

When Graham reached the age of seven I had my laundry flapping its vans on the double clothesline in the front side yard or the side front yard, partly for practical reasons and partly in celebration made possible because I have some things gay enough for the purpose. Graham and I were both gay. The sun was up even earlier than we were, and its warmth and light came pouring down.

It seemed a chancy thing back there when Graham was

a puppy of a few weeks and I almost seventy-five years old, and we undertook the adventure of living together. The great question remains unanswered — how nearly will our life spans come out even? Who will go away and leave the other alone? Let that great question go while we deal with small ones. Whatever may happen, Graham and I have had seven years of companionship.

I have a word of explanation about my laundry out there in the breeze (northwesterly, a good drying wind). When I was in primary school, with my special talent for making no sense out of instructive and decorative poetry, one poem I particularly failed to understand was Browning's "Incident of the French Camp," which begins, "You know, we French stormed Ratisbon." The climax is reached when the heroic boy arrives, full galloping, and flings from his horse at the mound where Napoleon is standing. "So tight he kept his lips compressed, Scarce any blood came through," as the boy announced, "The Marshal's in the market-place / And you'll be there anon / To see your flag bird flap his vans / Where I, to heart's desire, / Perched him! . . ."

I had no idea what a flag bird was, and "vans" stumped me completely. *The American Heritage Dictionary* allows, as a third definition, "*Archaic.* Any winnowing device, as a fan." I think Browning was stretching things. Even the word "perched" made no sense to me in this context, and I was unmoved when "smiling, the boy fell dead."

I will own that I suffered also from the obscurity of "Pippa Passes." If the year was at the spring, I thought it must be the same kind of spring as the one in a mossy glen at North Tisbury where we got water in times of drought. The word "at" implied geography, a place, and a physical presence to be at the place. I did understand "dew-pearled" and thought it offensive.

All this explains why my laundry is flapping its vans in honor of Graham's seven years.

Most of our joint affairs, Graham's and mine, have been made up of small encounters. We had one only the other day. A rough-coated girl dog, spaniel-type, about half Graham's size, lives around the corner in Cottage Street. Her name is Maria. In the early morning she was lying on her front porch with nothing in the world to do and no plans for the day, but as Graham and I happened along, in the slightest breath of time Maria was full of importance. She brimmed over with importance.

She joined our walk, darting this way and that along the way with errands of her own. As we headed along Eel Pond Road she went off on forays, reporting back presently with gleaming eyes, and then quickly pursued some creature or idea with a consuming air of purpose. Even when she was out of sight Graham and I knew she was a member of our walk, and this made all the difference.

When we walked back through Cottage Street, Maria resumed her position on her front porch, obviously with nothing to do and no plans for the day. I felt, though, that things would turn up, as something already had. We enjoyed several more walks with Maria before she moved to Ocean Heights with her family for the summer.

Graham, no matter who may be with us, attends to his own checkpoints and interests. Each of his pauses may be put down as an encounter, though with what, it is not my business to know. It is certain he encounters *something*. The rite of a dog's lifted leg belongs securely in the custom of our lives and must concern some significant recognitions. A book was presented for my inspection in which an expert elucidated the whole rite or procedure in terms of territory and aggression. This expert, I thought, was a B. F. Skinner on the subject, severely extrinsic and taking pains to go beyond freedom and dignity. I did not believe a word in the book and thought it complete nonsense.

The expert had relied upon patterns discerned in acts of single dogs. How would he spread his theory to cover walks with any or all the following, en route together: Graham, of course; Ellie, the setter who is allowed to lie on my couch; Scheherazade, the afghan loaned to us by Barbara Nevin; Benny Too, border collie of the Harry Weiss family; Tenny, short for Ten Eyck, the yellow Lab whose puppies I raised in my kitchen; and, though she has walked with us only a couple of times, Missy, a Yorkshire belonging to Margaret Patch.

Five is usually the limit of the number of dogs on a single walk; more than that tend to form splinter groups. My view is that the markings they leave on posts, rocks, and so on, if indeed marking is the purpose, incline to be random. There is no overall configuration. Territorial claims or notifications would make no sense whatever.

A better hypothesis is that we have here a phase of dog culture. The definition of "culture" in *The American Heritage Dictionary* is simpler than Dr. Daniel Bell's: "The totality of socially transmitted behavior patterns, arts, beliefs, institutions" and so on. The word "human" is interjected, but this is a human dictionary. I would adapt the definition to a concept of dog culture by analogy rather than by resemblance. Words such as "synoptic," "conceptual," "phantasmagoric," and "interdisciplinary" do not seem out of place here.

There is also the ceremonial aspect, and this has its counterpart in human behavior, as one recognizes in reading, say, *Tristram Shandy*, Tobias Smollett's *The Expedition of Humphry Clinker*, or Aldous Huxley's *Chrome Yellow*, in which Mr. Wimbush puts his privy on an upper floor in order to elevate a lowly function.

This is all incident to a tempting explanation, but I am aware that both we and our dogs live in a world of doubt; therefore I refer to that rule of an earlier experimental scientist, known to students as Lloyd Morgan's Canon, warning that we should not assume exercise of a higher psychical faculty when the exercise of a lower one fits the circumstances as well. Not that any of us knows in the life of dogs which is higher and which is lower, but I will settle for the explanation that dogs do what they do because it is fun. If this does not undercut the B. F. Skinners, I don't know what will.

Tenny, the yellow Lab, came into our lives when she was a puppy of a few weeks. Her master, Peter Brooks, played tennis with Edie Blake, and Tenny would sport around the courts, striking up an acquaintance with Graham. Sometimes when Peter was in Boston or Cambridge, Tenny would stay with Edie Blake and her parrot, Coco, and occasionally Graham and I would take Tenny for walks. I remember a long one in pouring rain in the rough country near the Eel Pond.

When Peter Brooks finally went to the Pacific Coast for the winter I said I would receive Tenny into our household with Graham and myself. Besides my acquaintance with Tenny so far, there was the fact that as a boy I had spent a night with my parents in the Ten Eyck Hotel in Albany. This seems a slender association, but it would suffice many a sportsman for betting some thousands on a horse of that name.

Tenny settled in well, much of the time with Ellie, who

had been properly spayed. There was a halcyon period of morning walks in Sheriff's Meadow and beyond, to the Harbor Light, alongshore, and in the woods at North Tisbury. Then I had occasion to recall what Peter had told me about Tenny coming into heat, and how accommodations had been reserved for her for the necessary period at Sonny Jackson's Shady Oak Kennels. All I would have to do would be to call Sonny.

Well, there's really no suspense to this story. I called Sonny and he said his kennels were full up, and how imminent was the occasion with Tenny. How did I know? I asked Edie Blake because of her experience with female dogs.

"Graham will tell you," she said.

But events crept up on Graham as they did with me. Graham lacks nothing in maleness nor in amatory ideas, else why did he let out a melancholy, despairing howl at precisely five minutes of two on Wednesday morning, all on account of a lady dog almost six blocks away at the corner of North Water and Cottage? But, as I have learned since, a male dog living in the same house as a female is likely to adapt gradually rather than suddenly to her changing condition. I should have had an outside arbiter, but I didn't know enough.

One critical weekend I realized that the peace of my household was definitely in hazard. I called Sonny Jackson again, and after questioning me he said he thought Tenny would be all right through Sunday. On Monday morning he said, "Bring her up this afternoon."

I did take her up Monday afternoon, but meantime there had been a tryst in the bushes somewhere beyond the Sheriff's Meadow Pond dike. We went for a final walk,

Tenny, Graham, Ellie, and myself. Ellie ran off about her business, probably concerned with black mud in some swamp hole. Tenny walked across the plank over the cut through the dike, and kept on going. Coming along after her with a determined, purposeful stride was Bo'sun, the golden retriever of the Sam Warriners. I blamed Bo'sun for what happened, but obviously he was too late, because in the litter of puppies all were black except for two ginger-colored. Golden Labs and yellow Labs are genetically interchangeable, but in this case I had to own that an outsider had been the sire.

It happened that Peter Brooks could be on hand — a holiday trip — for Tenny's labor. It was he, sitting up all night in the Brooks kitchen, who delivered seven live puppies and one stillborn. I was so relieved to have Peter discharge this responsibility that I was almost complacent when the litter was delivered to me and put in a whelping box in the kitchen. Jane Brown generously lent us that ultimate necessity, the whelping box. I had forgotten, if I ever knew, that puppies don't have their eyes open for about a week. I felt better when that week was past.

Tenny, of course, attended to her duties of feeding and licking, and she also indicated a dutiful protective jealousy for a day or two. She kept her eyes on the clock. What she really wanted was to get out with the gang. She romped with Graham and Ellie. She did remember that she had puppies, because she returned to the kitchen to feed them, but I had expected from her a greater sense of responsibility.

A kitchen is a good, practical, and impossible place in which to have a whelping box and seven growing puppies with an on-and-off mother. Ellie and Graham remained aloof. I was the one who cared, while Tenny became more and more the dog who had come to dinner.

The one duty to which she gave close attention was eating. The rules said she must be fed every two hours, right through the weaning period. Graham and Ellie, who showed up regularly to see what was going on, had forgotten their puppyhood and had not realized that it was possible for dogs to be fed oftener than twice a day — light breakfast and full dinner. The discovery of Tenny's schedule was as exciting as the discovery of fire was to Prometheus. (I am aware that the fame of Prometheus rests on his theft of fire, but he must have discovered it beforehand.) Since there was something as good as that around, Graham and Ellie wanted to be in on it too.

I decided desperately and improvidently that it would work out to the same end if I fed these two their usual quantity, but in smaller segments and oftener. They were not really put off with three times a day, but I made this schedule stick. They settled for it and punished me in their own way, until things leveled off. Now, although neither would dream of begging for my food when I was at the table, they saw no harm in begging for their own food. When Graham put his forefeet in my lap and directed his brown eyes at some point beyond me, I understood and he understood it was dog rations he wanted, but a stranger could be pardoned for thinking perhaps he hoped to share what was on my plate. I disliked this confusion of facts by misinterpretation.

Before the adoption process was completed, with good homes found for all the puppies, my dining room as well as kitchen had been turned over to the urgent need for more space and better facilities for exercise. I had long needed a new dining room rug, and I did not regret the passing of the old one, especially considering the state it was in; yet in ordinary course the old one would have done me for years more, and I might even have bought a television set instead of a new rug. When the puppies had gone, without any distress on Tenny's part, and when at last she was gone, Graham and I settled back into the best copy we could manage of the life we had lived before.

The grown-up Graham at seven is surprisingly like the young Graham of as many months. At times when he stands beside me on some knoll or headland, I glance down and wonder at the searching character of his gaze. He does not look into the future, for his whole life is in the present, as mine should be and nearly is, but with his head erect, jaws parted, eyes intent, and in an attitude of close attention, I think he must see and smell afar, and that he must be arriving at wise judgments. The next moment he is likely to pick up a stick and play with it, or march proudly with it, showing that he isn't all that grown-up or all that wise. Sometimes he will pick up a branch from a tree, so big he can hardly manage it, and will expect to carry it through an aperture not half the measure of the branch. Failure to negotiate such a passage does not dismay him a bit, and in this at least he has genuine wisdom.

If I sneeze he rushes to attend me instantly, wherever I am, and preferably to jump upon me, as he has done since his puppyhood. On all such occasions I must stop and show my appreciation of his guardianship and care. Sometimes when I am at the typewriter upstairs I sneeze heedlessly, not thinking, and if Graham happens to be in the kitchen I hear him scrabbling across the kitchen floor, then a muted rush across the new rug in the dining room, a whirlwind turn into the hall, and up the stairs he comes at his most furious speed.

Nowadays he has a wider choice of ways to ask me to let him out, even one recent morning standing beside my bed and howling like the hound of the Baskervilles. All the time his tail was wagging and his eyes were smiling. I got out of bed, went downstairs with him clumping after me, and let him out. I watched through the window and saw him lie down contentedly in the starlight. I suppressed a subliminal wish to join him, but there is no way someone like me can make primal use of the starlight between dark and dawn.

Graham's attitude toward those large dog biscuits known as Milk Bones has changed. At first he wanted me to know that he was not taken in by them. Later he would accept one and bury it in the yard, not deeply, but at an ecological level under leaves or litter. Now he likes to devour one or two ceremonially at precisely the same spot on the new rug. Ellie eats hers wherever she happens to be. Ellie, I am sorry to say, has a weight problem.

Besides scaring off certain plumbers, delivery men, and the laundry driver, Graham, with Ellie's collaboration if she happens to be on the premises, raises a sustained, alarmist vociferation whenever the United Parcel Service truck appears in the neighborhood. It is too massive and magisterial to miss barking at, and at times the truck makes a stop both at the Pierce Lane and Sheriff's Lane side of our premises, with a resultant galloping back and forth with raucous outcries. People unversed in dog knowledge ask me why Graham dislikes the UPS truck. He doesn't dislike it — he relishes and celebrates its appearances. All dogs enjoy repetitions, the return of the recog-

nized, the fulfilled expectations — just as we also enjoy
finding a pattern in our lives.

This is not to suggest an identity of dog and human
zests and experiences, but perhaps another analogy. I am
not sure how Graham's understanding may be assessed or
interpreted. What I do know is that he would understand
everything if he could, in my terms as well as in his own.
The willingness, the eagerness overflows in Graham's alert
brown eyes, the movement of his plume — his expressive
tail — the angle at which his ears are posed. He knows
what he is about, and he would like to know, even if only
for his own purposes, what I am about.

He does know places and their names and expresses his
own preferences, and this alone is a secure basis of our
companionship. To be without a dog is worse than being
without a song, but here I am interpreting my own behavior and emotions and transposing them to Graham's
willingness to understand and share. I think the earliness
of our days suggests to him, as to me, an earliness of life
and a predictable renewal without which both of us would
be deprived. We both love what we have and hope to have
more of it.

No, Graham does not hate the UPS truck. There is not
much hate in Graham's life because there has been so little
occasion for it. He experienced no hate when we had the
fight with Fluff, the young Saint Bernard, at the corner of
the tennis court one gray winter morning before dawn. I
say "we" because I was in it to the extent of floundering on
the ground while Graham and Fluff went to it, but I really
added nothing to the hostilities.

Fluff, who had grown rapidly from an engaging puppy
to a powerful young adulthood, was mistaken if he thought

he had acquired territorial rights. Graham responded to Fluff's challenge, and they were at it, furiously. I don't know why Fluff withdrew, but he did, and I got up from the ground and wondered exactly where we were. It took a while to find out.

Graham had been bitten in the leg, a matter that had to be attended to by the veterinarian later in the morning. His leg is about his only vulnerable spot; almost all the rest of him is protected by mouthfuls of rough hair. I wouldn't say that Graham lost, and I know he didn't think so.

A man who has the run of the house without a woman to regulate it tends to spread himself out, and often I sit on Graham's bed in his room when I put on my shoes in the morning. Almost always at such times Graham enters, bounds upon the bed, and lies there making small, interesting sounds. He isn't asking for anything, or complaining, or expressing any logical opinion. He is just talking in a confidential way while we relate to each other, joined in a communication at least as intelligible as the average of telephone conversations.

My shoes are soon tied, the interlude is over, and down the stairs we go for breakfast, outdoors, and the walk that begins another day.

THE LETTERS agreeing with us and advising us in the McDonald's affair kept coming for a good while, reaching into June and the beginning, at long last, of the hearings — for the plural was now necessary — in our Harbor View case. The hearings extended in their turn into late June, July, and August.

One of the McDonald's letters was from Ralph Arlyck, who told of his documentary film, *Hyde Park — America on the Hudson*:

> In one sequence we watch Franklin D. Roosevelt, Jr., lovingly place flowers on his parents' graves. He then leads the viewer to Route 9 and points out where the sale of land across the highway by his brother Elliott led to strip development of apartments, motels, gasoline stations, fast-

food franchise operations and other attractions teasing motorists into their asphalted yards with nationally standardized graphics and familiar creature gratifications. Great are the wounds to tradition and place that this form of prosperity has inflicted. The prospects of profit have pitted more than one man in Hyde Park against his brother.

Mr. Arlyck wrote that "one of the major scenes (in fact some think the best) . . . is the one in which McDonald's seeks zoning approval for a franchise in town." He described the scene:

We watch well-meaning attempts at curbing development. For instance, the McDonald's Corporation comes to a town hearing and presents an understated restaurant without the familiar double ditto copy of the St. Louis Gateway Arch. In return for this concession, McDonald's is given permission to chain-saw massacre a stand of giant pine trees wedged in between a gas station and a motel in the center of the village. Perhaps, like woolly mammoths, the trees have lived longer than the climate that has sustained them. The film illustrates that such changes are not the devastating single-strokes of land barons; they are, in fact, little changes that become raveled into the evolving fabric of the community.

Another belated letter, this one of the most interesting, came from Durango, Colorado, written on two sheets torn from a notebook, in what I took to be a youthful hand:

I just read a thought-provoking article in the *Durango World* concerning your community's battle with McDonald's. I was touched by your desire to keep the special flavor of your island, although I have never been there. I can relate a similar experience that happened in Durango.

Durango is the home of the last narrow-gauge trains in the world, and we play host to 120,000 passengers from Durango to Silverton, a mining town high in the Rockies.

Durango has many old hotels and businesses, and the essence of the train station's district is out of the 1890s.

McDonald's promised to maintain the western style in its restaurant, which they built next to the train tracks, across from the station. Now, the building was looking fine — rustic, etc., etc. UNTIL they put up the arches (small ones, they promised) and the neon lights on the roof, and it's just disgusting.

I wish I had money to help with, but please accept my moral support instead. If you don't want Ronald McDonald on your island, fight it and fight it, because even if they promise a white clapboard fishing shack decor, they will end up building a nice white clapboard with red and yellow neon signs.

Well, I don't like McDonald's hamburgers anyway.

We stored these communications away against some possible future need, when Ralph Arlyck's Hyde Park documentary and the testimony from Durango may help Martha's Vineyard repel one or another fast-food purveyor.

◠

There never was to be an agreed statement of facts in the Starbuck's Neck case, probably because attorneys on both sides saw some advantage — or at least no disadvantage — in delay. We were, anyway, taught that one American freedom is that nobody really has to agree with anybody — outside of court.

But now came a letter from Andrew Newman, Esq., of the Harbor View counsel, to Charles Corkin II, sometimes known around Boston as "Bud" Corkin, hearing officer for the DEQE, suggesting that we get on with the business.

"Dear Mr. Corkin," the letter began, "I am afraid that if this case continues in its present state it will be filled with letters with charges and countercharges between lawyers. While this exchange goes on, my client, Harborview Hotel Co., Inc., is being deprived of a hearing and a decision in this matter." (In its corporate identity the hotel used this form, "Harborview," rather than the historic and familiar "Harbor View.")

Even this letter was not urgent, but it moved in the direction of urgency. Had the hotel company waited for Edgartown to withdraw from the Martha's Vineyard Commission? Edgartown had withdrawn. Had we waited in the hope that Edgartown would vote itself back in? It wouldn't.

The question was raised whether regulations of the commission, the regional body of which Edgartown had been a member, could still have force now that the town had withdrawn. An affirmative answer could be decisive in the Harbor View case. It was first raised concretely when a Connecticut land company projected eight half-acre lots on Herring Creek Road with entrance driveways plotted at distances of every 200 feet. This plan was upsetting because of the small lots, the closely spaced driveways entering a main road, and a safety hazard involving the nearby Katama airport. The Edgartown Planning Board invoked the highway district regulations of the Martha's Vineyard Commission to prevent the development, but a superior court justice, in a declaratory judgment (which meant that no arguments were heard) ruled the regulations could no longer be enforced. The town appealed, both Planning Board and selectmen taking part, a notable irony, but the result of the appeal was nothing to wait up for.

In the Harbor View case our attorney, Jerry Healy, having gone into teaching and private practice, we retained young Gregor I. McGregor, an aggressive conservation lawyer, and through him the services of young specialists in a firm called Interdisciplinary Environmental Planning (IEP), who represented the fields of biology, geology, ecology, and planning.

DEQE procedure requires submission of written testimony, to which nothing may be added later, and cross-examination of the witnesses by opposing attorneys. The restriction against later information, no matter how relevant, baffled Lane Lovell and myself, and we went to Boston on behalf of our citizens' group. Questions were asked that we could easily have answered, but were prevented because the information had not been in our original testimony.

My intended testimony had been virtually pre-empted by events of the morning of January 25, 1979, when Graham and I had arrived at Starbuck's Neck to find a wind-driven sea sweeping over the wetland and churning against the bank. Only a few ridges and thicketed islands stood above the turmoil of rain and breaking waves. The thunder of surf on the east beach of Chappaquiddick added to the intensity of the storm, and the ocean poured into the harbor like an enormous river, breaking into white crests whenever it met an obstacle. When the sky had lightened, a little past seven, Edie Blake, who is a professional photographer, photographed the scene as it then was, though the wind had dropped and the tide had fallen considerably.

This was excitingly new to our case, and we could not know that Mr. Corkin would look at the pictures and decide that they were of no relevance whatever. New to our case also was the discovery by the town's marine biologist that the lagoon was well populated with the clams known as "steamers" and with quahaugs, which include in an early stage of their development the littlenecks of banquet halls and restaurants. The lagoon area would be too small for a commercial shellfishery, but it offered an excellent ground to be fished under family permits. Garry Hollands of IEP substantiated the town biologist's report.

So now, in mid-June 1979, Lane Lovell and I were off to Boston by plane, heading for the parasol of smog that identified the city. We found Greg McGregor in his law office in one of the historic narrow red-brick buildings of Beacon Hill, but Greg led us directly to the twenty-ninth floor of One Federal Street, occupied by the law offices of Davis, Malm and D'Agostine. Beacon Hill was quite one thing, and this was quite another.

The parquet floors shone, modern oriental rugs were aflash with bright color. Sedate old prints hung on the walls, and also uncommunicating modern art forms of a proud style. A grandfather's clock stood near the entrance, and on the anteroom table a symbolic discarded *New York Times*, properly standard equipment for a busy and prosperous urban law office. Glass partitions shone and an attractive young woman seated at an electric typewriter smiled a good morning and offered her assistance. The hearing room, immediately at hand, looked through outside windows upon long, remote vistas of old Boston.

Mr. Corkin, a former assistant attorney general now employed on a per diem basis, appeared at eleven o'clock, an hour at which I was accustomed to consider the best part of the day already spent. I could understand why he was called "Bud." He was young enough for that, but he embodied the law and an authority of official function.

"Let me do something that I have not done in the past,"

he began. "I don't believe the opponents can win this case here before the commissioner or before the courts, based upon the law as it exists today, and I'll tell you why, and then I'm going to ask you whether or not you want to proceed with the cross-examination. You're obviously entitled to that."

We, of course, were the opponents, and Mr. Corkin stood for the time being in the position of the commissioner of the DEQE.

"The case as I see it," Mr. Corkin went on, "based upon the expert testimony, deals with two neighbors trying to protect two home builders from themselves, and I don't think the statute permits the state to allow this to happen."

Of course this was not the fact. Mr. Corkin chose the unlikely interpretation that we citizen interveners, fourteen in number, and only two of them neighbors of the Harbor View, were going to all this effort and expense to protect "home builders" Robert J. Carroll and his partner Allen M. Jones from building structures in the wetlands in defiance of their own interests. None of us had any such concern. As recently as 1975, the case already begun, the wetland had been offered for sale for $350,000, indicating that the term "developers" or "entrepreneurs" would have been more accurate than "home builders," this latter striking us as a propaganda touch.

Mr. Corkin continued: "Land as close as that to the ocean is apparently subject to flooding, any land subject to the ocean, and we don't need a very sophisticated procedure such as this to make that proof . . ." Yet one of the seven interests of the Wetlands Act required a distinction among shorefront sites acceptable for development and others at which flooding hazards were too great.

"If you're in front of the ocean, the people who own the

Harbor View have to know if they spent some time in their own hotel, that that land is wet," Mr. Corkin went on. "I've looked at the photographs and I believe all the testimony about the water being there, but I don't think the law permits the state to say no to these people based upon the evidence . . . The state has the right to tell them how to build it so it won't blow away, but I don't think it has the right to tell them they can't build it."

Mr. Corkin had retreated from the word "flooding," used in the text of the law, to the milder words "wet" and "water."

He recognized Mr. Rudman, senior counsel for the Harborview corporation, who allowed himself a playful moment: "I would like to have all of your statement changed in that where it says the statement was made by Charles Corkin, I would like it to appear a statement made by Stanley Rudman, because you took all the wind out of my sails, and I don't see that any hearing officer has a right to do that."

"Well, I've been a hearing officer before," said Mr. Corkin. "Thank you for coming, anyway." Then he suggested that we take a break and decide whether we, Lane Lovell and I and the other citizen interveners, would go forward. "Obviously," Mr. Corkin added, "I could predict that you'd believe I'm right."

His prediction was wrong. We took the break and we voted not to quit, despite Bud Corkin's warning that we might be getting ourselves into "a process that could be weeks. In fact it's likely to be months of trial, which is a very costly venture to you, to the proponents, and in this particular situation to the state as well. So I just want you to know my views. It is not a prejudiced view."

I hope I have written nothing to lead any reader to expect an impending resolution of our case, for it still lies pretty much within the range of Mr. Corkin's warning, though we hope not to the extreme of Jarndyce and Jarndyce in *Bleak House*.

I have come to understand better the procedures under the Wetlands Act after considering a newsletter of the Massachusetts Association of Conservation Commissions, perhaps occasioned in part by our case which is, at least, referred to.

"The issue central to the problem is the wording of the Wetlands Protection Act itself," the newsletter begins, and goes on:

> Careful reading of the act shows that wetlands, in and of themselves, may not be protectable, but rather the "interests" of the act — public and private water supply, groundwater supply, flood prevention, storm damage prevention, prevention of pollution, fisheries and land containing shellfish — are protectable. This interpretation of the act introduces an element of schizophrenia into wetlands protection. It allows wetlands to be totally destroyed so long as the values of that wetland, as listed in the act, are replaced with some type of engineering solution.

What puzzled me now was how convinced environmentalists, such as the DEQE attorney professed himself to be, with obvious sincerity, should expend his skill and energies to uphold the "interests" of the act and the engineering solutions, and to defeat the interests of ecology and the environment.

The June hearing ground along to a 4:30 P.M. conclusion, too late to permit Lane Lovell and myself to board a plane homeward, so we took a bus to Woods Hole and crossed Vineyard Sound on the next to the last ferry, which was very late indeed.

Since then, with further hearings, we have accumulated five transcripts of testimony amounting in all to 603 type-written pages. We have established that the shellfish in the lagoon receive food from the Harbor View wetland, but I heard Mr. Corkin say — this at a hearing in Edgartown — that he wanted to know how much food a clam needed to eat. It is suggested that those in the lagoon can get along without the contribution from the nearby wetland.

∽

"Have you been out to Katama lately?" The question was put to me by one friend after another with an undertone unmistakably ominous.

Out to Katama, about two miles from the center of Edgartown, the margin of the outwash plain, our own Great Plain, where Mattakeesett Bay lies on the east and the Atlantic ocean roars in from south and west, or at times, in the words of the poet, "like a cradled creature lies." The Mattakeesett herring creek runs a mile from the bay to the Great Pond, and seaward of the creek the dunes begin, or what has been left of them by the hurricanes that began a great destruction in 1938. The region of Katama had always seemed elemental, timeless, reverently natural, and never to be claimed by any work of man.

"No," I said to my friends, "I've not been out to Katama lately."

"Then don't go." Each friend repeated the warning.

But the warning would in any case have made it certain that I would go, even if I had not already become aware of invading "development" replacing the historic isolation. I knew I must see for myself what turned out to be a multiplication of identical alien houses, annoyingly close to and at odds with one another, an imposture of design both pretentious and grotesque.

Today's memories do not go back as far as the ambitious era of the old Katama hotel, Mattakessett Lodge, on the bay side of the plain, but I have seen the hundred-year-old advertisements showing a comely building in the manner of a chateau, an octagonal tower at one end and a high mansard gable at the other. What would I have thought, I wondered, if I had come suddenly upon such a creation in the old French style?

"Katama the Lovely," said the advertisements announcing the opening of the lodge, "kept by Mr. Stumcke," with "the famed Atlantic Beach, beyond which there is no land for thousands of miles. The constant rolling of the surf fascinates all beholders, and after a storm is impressively grand. Daniel Webster declared it superior to Niagara. The mountainous wave crests, many miles in width, topple and fall with a noise like thunder . . ."

I do not know what I would have thought of this at another time; I suspect that a certain wistfulness would have been aroused and satisfied. One thing, though, is certain. The trap was set long ago, and when conditions were right the jaws would close. Not only the lodge at Katama but some of the other developments were aspirations of an honest fancy, and they had, like fashions and excesses of ambition, a short life. What was to be dreaded now was permanence, an irreversible course of economic determinism and destruction of resources by the unrestrained pressure of population growth and demand.

The enormities are what drive home the lesson of the

times, and Chappaquiddick has one too, a massive concretion of a building that, seen from a distance, possesses nothing but mass and height above the moors. As a modern house it has been pictured and acclaimed in a lifestyle magazine, but on the moors it is a bastille beyond the power even of the mightiest storms to bring to earth.

Professor Shaler of Harvard, one of the visitors quoted earlier, advised Americans to see this part of their country unspoiled while they could. At the turn of the century an Edgartown directory listed forty-four owners of summer homes, including Colonel Charles J. Allen, who had built that first cottage at Starbuck's Neck, and fourteen renters of houses or cottages for seasonal occupancy. The Home Club presented a membership roll of summer visitors intermingled with resident merchants, professional men, and retired sea captains.

There were shared activities: illuminated boat parades, catboat regattas, entertainments in the town hall; but when Betty and I arrived in 1920 the new motion picture house on Main Street was nearing completion, and it was becoming hard to tell whether summer sojourners were visiting the old Edgartown or a summer colony of their own creation.

Soon there were airplanes flying in and out. Automobiles changed old ways of life. Insularity no longer meant aloofness, and certainly not isolation. Developers and speculators, the entrepreneurs of population growth, had worked their will on Cape Cod and now discovered the innocence of Martha's Vineyard and the possibilities of its open land.

The change must have been less gradual than it now seems. The National Park Service report of 1964, brought about by John B. Oakes, saw the danger of "unbridled subdivision and the inroads of tasteless commercial exploitation" beginning on the Island. The 1969 report of Metcalf and Eddy to the Dukes County Planning and Economic Development Commission saw the time of grace rapidly closing in and a clear and present danger to the county, "one of the few bastions of rural environmental splendor left along the coastline of the eastern coastline of the United States." In 1972 came the Kennedy Bill to forestall the intense developmental pressure on the Nantucket Sound Islands that had irretrievably destroyed parts of our national heritage.

"Can you be the exception . . . ?" the Metcalf and Eddy report had asked of the residents of the County of Dukes County. The rest of the challenge was clear enough: ". . . and protect the rural environment of your county from the ravages caused by unrestricted development, or will your failure to act decisively and rapidly result in the indeterminate destruction of natural resources, as has happened elsewhere?"

"Can you be the exception . . . ?" But the exception to what mode of thought and conduct, to what vision of the future?

Dr. Daniel Bell's definition of modern middle-class society seems as good an answer as any: ". . . institutionalized expectation of economic growth and a rising standard of living; a change of values into a sense of entitlements . . . characterized not by needs but by wants which, since they are psychological, not biological, are by their nature unlimited." The engine of appetite, Dr. Bell observed, "is the increased standard of living and the diversity of products that make up so much of the splendid colors of life."

All this was a tremendous lot to declare oneself the exception to. Not "an" exception, but "the" exception. So good a thing going, and not to be a part of it!

Back in 1964, a long time ago as the world was moving, August Heckscher, who was then director of the Twentieth Century Fund, addressed Les Rencontres Internationales at Geneva, describing an urgent reality and offering a prophecy:

"To find nooks and crannies where a man can be alone will be more and more difficult . . . The result of technological forces combined with increased wealth, mobility and increased leisure, is to threaten the existence of every geographical place which is separate and distinct, every integrity which gives to the individual the possibility of standing apart and meeting the world on his own terms."

The trap was indeed set long ago. A little more than a hundred years ago a visitor on the Vineyard wrote to a Boston newspaper, "Some enterprising men will make princely fortunes here, in purchasing lands, soon in my judgment to be in demand."

He was ahead of his time. But years gradually filled the gap, and in the fall of 1979 the Edgartown Planning Board reported that there had been more than 500 subdivisions in the eighteen months just gone, and the lots had been aggressively marketed. The board asked a zoning code change from a half an acre standard to an acre and a half, lest two outlying areas be divided into 2300 lots, enough for an additional 8000 people in a town that only recently owned a resident population of 1400; but the proposed change failed to win a necessary two-thirds majority and the ultimate decision was postponed while development went on.

The jaws of the trap were closing, and so would come the destruction of the old Martha's Vineyard by many forces and many people, including petty officials and power blocs, special-interest groups, developers, and the Supreme Judicial Court of Massachusetts, which ruled that all real estate must be assessed at "full and fair market value," this at a time of unchecked inflation and speculative pressure on open land.

"What the individual requires," August Heckscher said, "is not a plot of ground but a place — a context within which he can expand and become himself. A place in this sense cannot be bought; it must be shaped, usually over a long period of time, by the common efforts of men and women. It must be given scale and meaning by their love. And it must be preserved."

But in this instant civilization of wealth and desire, what price a birthright or a heritage unless measured in the terms of material possessiveness?

In an *American Scholar* essay, René Dubos wrote: "Even in areas that have been plowed, bulldozed, built upon, there persist some stubborn peculiarities of the place that enable it to retain its identity — some local characteristics of the air and of the light despite the smog; a relationship between soil, rock, water and slopes despite manipulation by real-estate developers; an overpowering seasonal rhythm despite the promiscuous use of air conditioning; an awareness of the past despite the disappearance of landmarks and monuments."

This may suggest the best approximation of the Vineyard of the future, and as an Island the Vineyard has a better chance than most.

"On what private, 'rational' considerations, after all, should we make sacrifices to ease the lot of generations whom we may never live to see?" Robert L. Heilbroner, economist, teacher, and writer, asks this question in his book, *An Inquiry into the Human Prospect*. He gives as his view of the only possible answer "our capacity to form a collective identity with these future generations." But this on the Vineyard, which for three centuries held fast and close to such an identity, has been rejected in relation to the basic natural resource, land, which is at the heart of the Island's character and ultimate values.

The defeat of the Kennedy Bill cannot be accounted as other than a major disaster, the rejection of the final opportunity for self-determination. The bill's passage by Congress would have made all the difference. It succeeded in the Senate but had been so amended in the effort to win Island support that it lost even the votes of committed environmentalists in the House. Ironically, many lovers of Martha's Vineyard believed in the purposes of the bill but did not want them accomplished in this particular way.

In the future, of course, there will remain preserves and enclaves established by gifts or covenants and safeguarded by agencies such as The Trustees of Reservations (a Massachusetts conservation group of long lineage), the Massachusetts Audubon Society, the Vineyard Conservation Society, the Sheriff's Meadow Foundation, and others. A fund-raising campaign in the *Vineyard Gazette* made possible the purchase of Cedar Tree Neck, a splendid headland extending into Vineyard Sound, and some two hundred acres of ridges, woods, and marshes lying inland from the neck, by the Sheriff's Meadow Foundation. My brother and I, with cordial family approval, gave sixty adjoining acres on the west, including a quarter mile of beach, to enlarge the Cedar Tree Neck preserve. The appraised value of the property was high, but we were not giving money. We were giving land.

I drive out to Katama again to see the houses that so conspicuously identify the modern "development" of Martha's Vineyard. I reflect that the Island's storied continuity has been marked by many variations and styles of building and has, in fact, been described as a "journal" of changing needs and responses. This being so, and since architecture is one of the performing arts, I wonder if future critics may not see these present invasions as ingenious and admirable forerunners of a new seaside culture and style.

It was at Anne Simon's place at Menemsha in the late summer of 1979 that I met Eli Ginzberg again, among the guests on the broad porch. Anne's book, *No Island Is an Island*, a defense of the Vineyard, had figured in the Sargent Bill hearing, and since then she had written *The Thin Edge*, a challenge and summons to defense of the coast.

Dr. Ginzberg smiled as he saw me approaching, for he remembered, as I did, that question asked quite a while ago at Chappaquansett, "Has the decline of Martha's Vineyard been more or less rapid than you expected?" What followed now in the fading summer twilight was not an exchange of despairs. This scholar of the human condition in its many aspects, a deeply experienced observer, spoke of the many places he had visited, worldwide, and not long ago but recently. Of them all, he said, Martha's Vineyard had changed the least.

I spoke of the Island's shift from a productive economy to a service economy, to tourism, and I found him tolerant of that, inviting me to consider New York City. I spoke of the summer crowding, subdivisions, jams of traffic, vandalism, and all the rest. I mentioned the monster tour buses discharging their passengers for gulped chowder and sandwiches, and then taking them aboard again to roll along within closed windows in air-conditioned isolation over roads of an Island they had no opportunity to understand.

"Oh," he said, "they get something out of it."

His grasp of a greater whole encircled my own more limited outlook. I knew that, and I realized already that I was one of the travelers from another time whose journey had been long and who must end as a stranger. In this relaxed company on a Menemsha porch it came to me that the scene repeated earlier ones, new faces replacing old, and that what I recalled from the past was recurring in the summer present. The "local gods and goddesses" of chosen places, a phrase of August Heckscher's, do seem to have a way of hanging about or dropping in for visits.

On my drive back to Edgartown I reflected, as I had at times before, that my peculiar treasure lay in having lived in and belonged to generations antedating this modern world. Was I not blessed in having been brought up by a mother who was born in 1858? In my youth there were only occasional automobiles, no airplanes, no radios, and of course no television sets. The mounting block and hitching post in front of our house in New Bedford were not there for ornament. Welsbach gas burners were the novelty in lighting when I was a boy.

Moreover, our middle class neighborhood represented in its confidence and enlightenment the age I heard described many years later by Professor Carleton J. H. Hayes as that of the "benevolent bourgeoisie," the term spoken with a curl of his lip and a mocking smile. This was at Columbia in 1916 when Professor Hayes was soon to suspend his lecturing and don the uniform of an Army captain. Later still he became our ambassador to Spain, but by that time the age of the benevolent bourgeoisie had become a legend dimly remembered if remembered at all. I had learned much from him, including the fact, as I take it to be, that society is better understood when it is mocked.

In view of all that has happened, I think the years in which I was brought up are particularly susceptible to the ironic smile and curled lip. Yet I am glad, beyond any regret, that I am one — one of the last, as it happens — who can have known that deluded but innocent, generous, and happy time.

$\sim$

I met Milton Birch at the corner of Church Street, and we went together to the pancake breakfast at the Senior Center, which is in a separate building behind the police station. We entered a small, cheery room where two tables were set with four places each, brightly decorated tablecloths; knives, forks, and spoons glistening properly; syrup cruets; individual cups of applesauce; and chilled orange juice about to arrive from the kitchen.

We sat down with Manuel Santos and were joined by John Willoughby. Margot Moore, who is in charge of the center, wanted to know why I hadn't brought Graham. I said there might be other reasons but it was mainly because he was not old enough to be a senior.

Milton Birch taught art for many years before his retirement to Edgartown, and for many seasons he had vacationed on Chappaquiddick, where his family had put down deep roots. Manuel Santos had begun working at the age of eleven, he told us, delivering groceries in a wheelbarrow for Manuel Silva, Jr., the retired whaleman who owned the Summer Street Grocery and believed in heavy cargoes ashore and afloat. John Willoughby had commanded tankers in far seas and in a partial retirement had served a congenial tour of duty as master of the Chappaquiddick ferry.

When Betty and I first knew Manuel Santos, he had risen to be manager of Fred Metell's new hardware store in Edgartown, an enterprise that brought Charlie Call, owner of the established hardware store, back from his Florida vacation in a hurry to look after his fences. Most of Manuel's working life, though, he had served as cemetery commissioner and in the allied business of monuments. He said his legs had "given out" at last, the muscles so continuously stretched as he handled granite year after year.

All four of us began remembering people and customs of old Edgartown a generation or more ago, especially the characters who frequented Bill Cottle's pool room or were widely known around town, such as Harry Collins, who sold popcorn from a market basket he carried on his arm and volunteered contemporary information and quotations from Scripture.

So many little things came back in the glow of recollection, in a sort of moonlight such as one knew in childhood. Manuel told of buying some meat at Ginter's store, which had preceded the arrival of the First National chain, and finding the meat full of maggots. When he took it back to the store, expecting contrition and apology, the manager said, "Oh, that's nothing. I've got a barrelful like that out back."

We remembered Ernie Holmes with his cap, initialed O.T.L.F., which meant "old time left fielder," and how he played in the town band and worked in Mellen's grocery in a marketman's white coat. Toward the end of his career he found a zither at the town dump on which he liked to twang out loud notes on some street corner late at night.

The Chappaquiddick ferry in the old, simpler days, was a skiff rowed back and forth by Jim Yates, and one time some jokesters tied a rope to the skiff, weighting it so that it would not show on the surface, and watched while Jim, in mid-channel, pulled and pulled on his oars without getting any closer to Chappaquiddick Point.

We remembered Sid Gordon, self-styled "plastered plasterer," one of the best of workmen, whose dog would walk with him only when Sid was sober, and when Sid was otherwise, remained on the opposite side of the street. Sid worked only when he chose, and claimed with reason that his life was more successful than most and a lot happier.

So we breakfasted together, the four of us, and were enclosed in a privacy of our own, tightly surrounded by an invisible and impenetrable boundary that I suppose may be called "time." I compared our situation mentally to that of the Sargasso Sea, precisely bounded but entirely by water, the only sea in all geography thus set apart in this peculiar fashion. Like the Sargasso, we preserved our mysteries and isolation, though presently we walked out into the sunshine together as if through no barrier at all.

We, who could share the past together, now proceeded each to his own affairs, or if it so happened, in that final degree of liberation and independence, to his own serene lack of affairs.